**An Installment from the
Back to the Family Series**

THE
PAINS &
JOYS
OF RAISING BOYS

Preparing our sons for manhood,
because a boy raised wrong, becomes the wrong man!

CARLOS JOHNSON

© 2008 Carlos Johnson

Published by:
Back-2-The Family
Publishing
www.Back2theFamily.org

All scripture quotations, unless otherwise indicated, are taken from the Holy Bible, New International Version ® copyright © 1973, 1978, 1984 by International Bible Society. Scripture quotations marked (NKJV) are taken from The New King James Version (NKJV) of the Bible copyright © 1982 by Thomas Nelson, Inc. Scripture quotations marked as (NLT) are taken from the New Living Translation Holy Bible. New Living Translation copyright © 1996 by Tyndale Charitable Trust.

The name satan and associated names are not capitalized. We choose not to give him any preeminence, even to the point of violating grammatical rules.

Author: Carlos Johnson
Cover Design Team: Edward Bentley
Editor: Ann-Marie Morris

First U.S. Edition Year 1st Edition 2008

Johnson, Carlos

The Pains & Joys of Raising Boys

Summary: The Pains & Joys of Raising Boys takes an in depth look at what it takes to raise a boy to be a productive, positive part of society in the roles of husband, father, provider, and head of the household. Because a boy Raised wrong becomes the Wrong man!

10 Digit ISBN 1-934363-33-2 Perfect Bound, Soft Cover
13 Digit 978-1-934363-33-1 Perfect Bound, Soft Cover

1.   Christian Living, Relationships, Parenting Boys

2008921002

For current information about releases by Carlos Johnson
visit our web site: http://www.back2thefamily.org

Printed in the United States of America
V3 01 24 08

To Those Who Pushed Me

This book is dedicated to those like myself who pray and work to have the following testimony:

This is my beloved son, in whom I am well pleased. (Matthew 3:17, KJV).

I'd like to acknowledge those who made this book possible—those who sheltered me while I researched and wrote, such as the staff at the St. John's Golf and Conference center. Those who shaped and spanked me like Bernice and Arnold Brandon. And those who hugged, trained, encouraged, and inspired me such as my wife Melissa, Ann-Marie Morris, Nicole Parker, Pastor Christopher Brooks, and my Christian family support group.

Even though they all had different roles their collective input, all amounted to one great push!

Therefore, it is with the above people in mind that I say

"If you cannot win the race
push
the man in front of you so that
he breaks the world record."

Carlos Johnson

THE
PAINS &
JOYS

OF RAISING BOYS

CARLOS JOHNSON

Contents

Section 4. This is My Beloved Son In Whom I am Well Pleased!

Prologue

From me to you…

This book is different in its presentation in that every chapter is written with four assumptions:

1. *the reader agrees* the end goal is to raise a son who will posses the skills to live independent of his parents but always dependent on God.

2. *the reader agrees* that when human psychology, science, family tradition, or personal preference is in conflict with the Word of God, God's Word will be the final authority.

3. *the reader agrees* that families are under attack, and in order to prepare our sons for manhood, parents must be ready for parenthood!

4. *the reader agrees* there is an intentional, systematic war being waged against our sons by an external enemy; therefore, the battle should not be parent vs. child. Rather, the battle should be the entire family united against the external enemy.

Finally, in order for any battle to begin somebody has to… **sound the alarm!**

If the village is the place that raises the child, somebody better sound the alarm, because the village is under attack!

Sound the alarm, because Victoria's Secret is no longer a secret.

Sound the alarm, because underwear has become outerwear.

Sound the alarm, because the terms *Playa* and *Pimp* are now terms of endearment.

Sound the alarm, because our sons know more about courtrooms than classrooms.

Sound the alarm, because our daughters too quickly go from Barbies to babies.

Sound the alarm, because it won't be long before a prom queen's name will be Mark.

Sound the alarm, because our sons know more about probation than salvation.

Sound the alarm, because parents used to say, "Because I said so, and that is the end of discussion." Now young people say, "I don't want to," and that is the end of discussion.

Sound the alarm, because mothers have been deceived to believe that sons don't need fathers.

Sound the alarm, because fathers have been deceived to believe that they don't need families.

Sound the alarm, because grandmothers have to be mothers all over again.

Sound the alarm, because too many children spend

more time playing games of death than reading books of life.

Sound the alarm, because too many children can't pass their school tests or a drug test.

Sound the alarm, because young people know more about sex than about Jesus!

Sound the alarm, because the enemy is not BET, or MTV, the enemy is SIN!

Sound the alarm because it is wartime, and woe be it to the man or woman who acts the same way in wartime as he or she does in peacetime!

In All Thy Getting,
Get Understanding

I am a Man!
No You're Not!
Yes I am!

The Struggle

There is a roadblock, a mountain, a hurdle in the path as we undertake the challenge of raising our sons from boys to men. Contrary to popular belief, the biggest hurdle parents face is not dealing with a single-parent family, homosexuality, feminism, bad parenting, or gangster rap.

Our biggest hurdle [after orginal sin] which blocks our sons' p leading them from boys to men is the fact that our society won't or can't agree on what a "man" really is.

This country has no idea anymore about the building process it takes to become a man. We do won't even agree on what the final "man" looks like, sounds like, feels like, thinks like, acts like or even lives like! Therefore, too many families are blindly struggling to raise their boys into their own versions of "men."

In Dr. Martin Luther King's book, *The Measure of a Man*, he writes, "The question, 'What is man?' is one of the most important questions confronting any generation. The whole political, economic, and social structure is determined by the answer to this pressing question." He goes on to say, "But although there is widespread agreement in asking the question, there is fantastic disagreement in answering it."

Some time ago, due to my speaking schedule, I thought it would be wise to buy a home gym. My thought was that I could work out early and avoid the time wasted driving to the gym. When the equipment arrived, knowing that a "man" could build anything, I opened the box and began putting screws in holes. After what seemed like forever, I realized I could not assemble this "easy to assemble" product without following the instructions. And then, I realized that seeing a picture of what it should look like when I am finished would help. So I looked at the photo of the home gym on the box. Once I did that, I knew what the end product should be, and following the instructions was much easier.

That is what is going on today with most parents raising boys—there is no agreed upon set of instructions for the process. And many of us who are responsible for this awesome task of building a "man" have never seen an "authentic man" and are truly working under a blindfold.

What is a Man? And What is Manhood?

It has been said, "Manhood is the mountain-top outside of Boys-ville, and in order to move into Manhood one can no longer look, think, or act like a boy!" Others have said that manhood is the butterfly from the boyhood cocoon.

The older men in the barbershop used to say, "Boy, your maleness is inherited, but manhood is merited!" As I got older, I understood what that meant. It meant that I was male by default. And my maleness had nothing to do with my wisdom, my deeds, or choice. Because, the title of "man" had to be learned and earned.

Oftentimes at my parent workshops, I joke by saying, "My wife and I will know when my son has matured into manhood when his driver's license has a different address on it than ours." Although that comment fills the room with laughter, there are many parents in the audience who are praying for that day to come. However, even though that achievement is a major signal of independence and responsibility, a new address alone does not say "manhood."

If I were to ask the question to a group of men, you'd hear many different answers depending upon environment and upbringing. Some may say, "He is a man when he has reached a certain age." Others say, "When he has moved out from under his mom's roof and has his own car and apartment." And some believe that making a certain amount of money is attaining manhood. None of these things alone gives our boys their address in "the city of Manhood."

The question becomes, "Where does this manhood training take place?" In the book, *Lost Generation? Or Left Generation!,* Rev. Clarence Lumumba James, Sr. suggests there are four key institutions in American society that purport to teach boys how to be men: the street, the prison, the military, and college. He writes:

> Survival on the streets is a test comparable to survival skills in the rainforest; however, a boy trained in the streets becomes a dangerous man to his community. A boy raised in prison becomes a man who believes manhood is someone with the physical force to protect the physical integrity of his or her anal cavity. And prisons don't produce the kind of men needed to build healthy relationships. The third institution, the armed forces requires our boys to shut down critical thinking faculties. For a soldier must not reason but do or die. Lastly, although they start the manhood process, a boy in college has adolescence prolonged, for he still depends on mom and dad for food shelter and minutes on his cell phone.

Finally, he goes on to say:

> If the Church were to rise to the challenge, it would become the institute of manhood-training that we need it to be and would solve its own manhood deficit.

Although I agree with most of his assessments and recommendations, my money is on the family as *the* institution perfectly and purposely designed for **manhood training**.

According to "street code," the definition of a man is

based on extreme masculinity and the amoral values of street life: gaming, hustling, girl hunting, loud talking, liquor drinking, tricking, lying, stealing, disobedience to authority, and fighting. Finally, one must go to jail, survive, and return back to the streets with a list of prison "who's who" contacts and stories to tell.

If one were to believe everything he or she sees in the media, "men," as defined in gangster rap culture, are grimacing, over-sized, monosyllabic cartoons, instead of the complex individuals "men" actually are. Lyrics in a majority of mainstream rap songs depict an image of manhood as including multiple female partners, a violent criminal history, and extreme interests in material goods such as: cars, jewelry, and expensive alcohol. The main problem with this image, as most social scientists would agree, is that it is too one-dimensional to encompass such a complex being.

The Agreement

Therefore, since it is difficult to get agreement on what *manhood* is, why don't we start with where we agree. First, I think we would all agree it takes a boy to be born in order for there ever to be a man. Another way to put it is, a boy is the only thing that God gives us to make a man—no other substance or substitute will do.

Secondly, let's agree that there is *manhood*. There exist a distinction between being male and becoming a man. Being male only qualifies one for the class; it does not guarantee that one will graduate into manhood. If we can at least agree to these two basic facts then the "what a man is, how he acts, and when does he becomes a man" conversation can begin.

Okay, if you accepted my barbershop wit and the societal agreement that there is a state of *manhood*, let us begin the conversation about what a man is. For this trick I will move from barbershop and hip-hop to the wisdom from the R&B group *The Ojays* and Holy Scripture. In the song, *Family Reunion*, the responsibility of a father was described this way:

You know the family is the solution
To the world's problems today
Now, let's take a look at the family
In the family the father is like the head
The leader, the director

Not domineering but showing love, guidance
For everyone else in the family
Now, if we could get all the fathers of the world
To stand up and be fathers, that would be great

Then we have mothers
Who are the right arms of the father
They're supposed to do the cooking

Raise the children, do the sewing
And help the father to guide and direct

Then there's the son
The son, most sons are like imitators of their fathers
So, we're back again to the father
If he is guiding in the right way
The son is definitely gonna be alright

1 Corinthians 13:11, lets us know that not only is there a state of manhood, but most importantly, there is a distinction between a male child and becoming a man. Here Paul the Apostle is talking about love, and in verse ten says, "but when perfection comes, the imperfect disappears." But it's almost as if someone said, "Paul, how do you know you are a man?" Paul says "When

> When I was a child, I talked like a child, I thought like a child, I reasoned like a child. When I became a man, I put childish ways behind me.

I was a child, I talked like a child, I thought like a child, I reasoned like a child. When I became a man, I put childish ways behind me."

From 1 Corinthians, we know that unlike a male child, a *man* does not **speak** like a child anymore—the imperfect has gone away. He does not whine, pout, throw tantrums and have childish conversations. Unlike a male child, a *man* no

13

longer **thinks** and **understands** the same way. He reasons with maturity and conviction. He no longer thinks only of self, he now considers how his actions and decisions affect others in the process. Fleshly pleasure is not his base desire and the driving force behind all he does, as it would be for a child. Lastly, a *man* puts away **childish things**. This lumps whatever else we want to discuss into one final statement: A man puts away all the childish stuff!

The bottom line is, a man does not speak, think, or act like a child, that is how we can know he is a man. It is not so much what a man *is* that describes a man, but what a man *does* that qualifies him for manhood.

The following chart provides a few helpful distinctions

Man	Male
Is a teacher	Is a student
Is a producer	Driven by consumption
Gives to his community	Takes from his community
Makes things	Breaks things
Gets married and stays committed to one woman	Shacks up
Brings order	Brings chaos
Is self-led	Is a follower of a group
Has a life full of responsibilities	Has a life full of video games, music, clothes, and chasing women
Will raise his children and someone else's	Won't raise his own children.

between *man* and *male*:

Corinthians also clearly communicates that to pass the "man test," you need to demonstrate proof that you are no longer a child. Manhood is a process, transition, and arrival from inherited maleness to an earned destination of distinction and responsibility. This is communicated when Paul says, "but when I became a man…"

> Manhood is a process, transition, and arrival from inherited maleness to an earned destination of distinction and responsibility.

In the book, *Playing Through*, Mr. Earl Woods writes a letter to his son Tiger explaining his intentional training and involvement in Tiger's transition into manhood:

A letter to my son…

You are my little man. You are my treasure. God gave you to me to nurture and to grow and to develop. I always have had your interests first and foremost in my life, and they always will be. In fact, you mean more to me than life itself. I can remember when I taught you that it was okay to cry—that men can cry. It was not a sign of weakness, but a sign of strength.

That was part of the education and the legacy that I wanted to leave with you, that sharing and caring for

others is a way of life. And it is not to be taken lightly.
I pass on all my abilities to share and to care to you. I
realize that you have an infinite, higher capacity, and
capability to perpetuate this philosophy in our day's
world. I trust that I have given you the guidance and
love with which you can then execute that mission.
What God has in mind for you, I don't know. It is not
my call. It was my job to prepare you. I trust that I
have done the best job that I can. I know you will give
it your all. And you will be my little man forever.

Love,
Pop

The promise of future and long-term blessings for a
boy is first and foremost tied into his family and not any
other institution. Ephesians 6:1–3 makes this clear when
we read, "Children, obey your parents in the Lord, for this
is right. 'Honor your father and mother'—which is the first
commandment with a promise—that it may go well with you
and that you may enjoy long life on the earth."

The human experience was designed in such a way that
we would learn our future roles just by living life at home.
"Manhood training 101" was designed to start by a boy
honoring his father and mother and the rest of the training
would fall right in place.

Therefore, if we want to save our boys on any grand

scale, we must first resurrect, rebuild, and depend on our families. I know I can hear the crowd saying, "But what about the boys who don't have the original family set-up?" In the upcoming chapters, we will discuss and provide key answers and strategies for developing a boy into a man whether he has his dad at home or not. However, please note God's formula has not changed; a boy needs a man to become a man. Don't worry; there is still plenty of room in the city of **Manhood** for your son. We'll leave the light on for him.

Chapter 2

Boys: The Good, The Bad, and The Ugly

Now Cain said to his brother Abel, "Let's go out to the field." And while they were in the field, Cain attacked his brother Abel and killed him (Genesis 4:8).

In the past eight years, I have spoken to and trained thousands of parents in community organizations, corporations, schools, and churches around the country. One of the questions that I frequently ask parents at workshops is, "What is your child's potential?" From the time I began asking that question to the time of writing this book, every response that I have received from parents has been similar to, "My child has the potential to be a doctor," "My child has the potential to be a lawyer," or "My child has the potential to be a teacher…etc…etc."

Not one parent, grandmother, or nanny in eight years has ever said, "My child has the potential to be a killer!" Not one has ever said, "Mr. Johnson, my child could be a dope dealer or thief." Sometimes I want to say to the audience, "If your kids could not do any evil, I wonder whose kids are selling and using drugs, stealing, robbing, having sex, and killing?"

I only ask this question to audiences in an effort to sober parents up so they can be emotionally and spiritually prepared for whatever future battle may come from their son. I also ask so that we all can admit aloud what we already know in our hearts to be true—that all of our kids have the potential to sell drugs, use drugs, steal, rob, have sex, and yes, kill. All our boys have the potential to turn their backs on all that we have taught them, all that we stand for, and all that we believe in.

> All our boys have the potential to practice good, bad, or ugly behaviors.

All our boys have the potential to practice good, bad, or ugly behaviors. Because of this fact, I classify a boy's behavior in three categories depending on the severity and consistency of their behavior in any season in their life. Due to a boys training and maturity, it is possible for a boy to exhibit several behavioral seasons during his journey to manhood.

The Ugly

If a boy is consistently choosing to act evil, I classify his behavior as "ugly." (I know you were looking for a softer word in this age of tolerance but I just call it as I see it.) When boys in our society choose to behave ugly for a period in their life, I call it their "Cain Season" after Adam and Eve's son who committed the greatest evil against his brother.

In this season, our sons all around this country are persuaded, influenced, convinced, or just plain downright enjoy walking and living on the wild-side of life. The boys in the Cain Season for many reasons, or maybe only one reason, have come to the conclusion that they would rather hurt than help, punish than protect, steal than study, or worst—kill rather than be kind.

One such fifteen-year-old boy described to me at one of my workshops his "season of ugliness":

Steven: *Man-nn, we would just choose a house and go up in it!*

Me: *Did you not care if anybody was home?*

Steven: *Naw bro, if they was home, we did what we had to do. I got two bullet holes right here [as he pulls up his pant leg] from one house and the man was up and chased us and started shooting.*

Me: *What made you break in homes? That seems kind of dangerous to me.*

Steve: *It was fun, nothing to do, I needed money and I wanted to see if it was for me.*

Me: *Was it?*

Steve: *Naw, it was not me.*

Me: *Thank God!*

In the book, *Makes Me Wanna Holler: A Young Black Man In America*, Nathan McCall says, "Carrying a gun did strange things to my head. Suddenly I became very much aware that I had the power to alter the fate of anybody I saw. The greatest power on earth is the ability to give life. The next greatest power on earth is the ability to take a life—and who does not want to have power!"

> I had the power to alter the fate of anybody I saw. The greatest power on earth is the ability to give life. The next greatest power on earth is the ability to take a life—and who does not want to have power?

In the movie, *Juice,* rapper and urban legend Tupac Shakor, in his acting debut, played a young punk who found and fell in love with the power, or juice, he received over life and death by picking up a gun and using its ugly power to make others fear him. Who could ever forget that Monday, April 16, 2007 when the worst mass murder at a school was committed by another one of our sons, Seung-Hui Cho, a twenty-three-year-old student at the Virginia Tech campus in Blacksburg, Virginia.

On several occasions, I have come in contact with the ugly things that our boys can do. One day I arrived at Rogel, one of my favorite Detroit golf courses, and was told that no golf carts were available because local boys had set them all on fire the night before after they were told to leave the course grounds.

These are only a few examples of how our boys choose to do ugly things and enter their very own Cain Seasons.

However, no mother or father looks into the eyes of their son in the crib and sees a future thief or killer. No parent ever says, "I know my boy will grow up and live a life of ugliness. But if we are to plan, and prepare our sons for greatness, we must realize that our sons have potential for evil. We must be proactive in leading them to greatness and away from the ugliness that is possible for them and their generation.

I can see most of you now saying, "No way, not my son, he would never be a part of that ugly side of his generation. My son has his own room. We take trips every summer to expose him to the world. I buy him what he needs so he won't have to steal or kill for it!"

My response is: that is great, halleluiah, and you are probably correct. The probability of your son living an ugly life and entering a Cain Season is very low. However, let us not forget that Cain himself did not come from the ghetto—the wrong side of the railroad tracks, he was not in a gang, nor did he did listen to rap music. His parents were not poor or third generation welfare recipients. Adam and Eve walked and talked directly to God and God talked back, yet because of Cain's jealousy for his brother, he used his freewill to choose to do an ugly thing and become a murderer! Therefore, how do we in the twenty-first century take a hands-off approach and think that we parents do not have to protect our sons from thinking and doing evil? How can we think that our handsome boys could not have the potential to do wrong?

Bad

The second type of behavior is when our sons, consistently choose to act "bad." I call this season in a boy's life the "Sons of Eli Season."

Eli, who was very old, heard about everything his sons were doing to all Israel and how they slept with the women who served at the entrance to the Tent of Meeting (1 Samuel 2:22).

This season describes our sons who, because they are protected and pampered from the responsibilities and consequences of life, have become, at best, under-achievers. They are charmers and cheats, tricksters, and slicksters who find ways around any level of honest work. They are under-performers who refuse to use the opportunities and gifts that God has given them except for their own gain. They are bad; and even worst——they are allowed to be bad.

> Eli, who was very old, heard about everything his sons were doing to all Israel and how they slept with the women who served at the entrance to the Tent of Meeting
> (1 Samuel 2:22).

These sons of ours get into trouble at school, and dare you to call their parents because they know that the punishment won't be that severe. These sons of ours come to your home to pick up your daughter, smile and say, "Hello Mrs. Johnson. That is a lovely dress you have on. Are you losing weight?" Then they take your daughter out to the wildest party and get her drunk. These sons of ours don't do enough to go to jail, for those deeds are too risky and too much work. They do just enough wrong that we can still clean it up. They actually count on the fact that we love them enough to give them another chance. After all, they know we don't want them to end up like those in the "Cain Season."

The Good

By faith Moses, when he had grown up, refused to be called the son of Pharaoh's daughter. He chose to be mistreated along with the people of God rather than to enjoy the pleasures of sin for a short time. He regarded disgrace for the sake of Christ as of greater value than the treasures of Egypt, because he was looking ahead to his reward (Hebrews 11:24–26).

The final behavioral season is the season that we all want our sons to get to and stay in, and our prayer is that they won't ever go through the other seasons at all. This season is reserved for seriousness. It is when our sons have begun to discover what is real and what is a lie about life and then they choose to believe in the truth. Josh McDowell, author of *Beyond Belief to Convictions,* says it this way, "Although we need to fear what our kids could be tempted to do, we need to be more concerned with what our kids are led to believe." He knows, as I do, that once our boys believe they have something **to live for**, something that is more than just pleasure and popularity, we can almost count on them making the right decisions outside of our presence.

In this season, our sons begin to decide what is not only best for them, but, at the same time, they consider how their actions or behaviors affect others. This is the season when our boys act "good." I call this season in a boy's life the "Moses Season." When a boy enters this season, he is a pure joy to be around, he is fun to ride with in the car, he is a joy to come home to—he is a joy just to be around. This boy asks, "Mom, how was your day today?" and "Dad do you need any help?"

In this season, ours sons understand and care how their behavior at school affects our workday. They understand how having to replace clothes, leaving on lights, and bringing the car back on empty effects the finances of the family.

In this season, our sons understand that their life has purpose, and because of that, there are certain places, people, and practices that he cannot participate in. Therefore, he is willing to walk alone, sacrifice, and maybe even suffer for what he has come to understand as real success!

When I was in school, there was a kid in my class named Mike Rodgers. When we were young he was always the odd kid and we could never figure him out. He wore bowties and got his nails polished. He kept his hair groomed and would never play in the dirt. One day he got into an argument with one on the girls in our class and she said, "Mike, you are so conceited." Without pausing for breath or even blinking an eye, Mike responded like he was waiting all year for someone to say what she said. To this day, thirty years later, I can still hear his reply. "I am not conceited, I am just convinced. Those who think otherwise are just confused!" From that day on, no one, and I mean no one, ever challenged Mike again about his convictions.

> Having convictions is being so thoroughly convinced that something is absolutely true and good that you take a stand for it regardless of the consequences.

Having convictions is being so thoroughly convinced that something is absolutely true and good that you take a stand for it regardless of the consequences.

One of the problems that today's sons have inherited from us is a world that has very few absolutes. Today, there are very few things at all that we are willing to say is absolutely right or absolutely wrong. We have handed over to our sons a world of tolerance and situational ethics. But if we want our sons to be "good" and live long in the "Moses Season," we must me willing and bold enough to set some standards for them to follow.

CHAPTER 3

Two Powerful Attacks on Our Boys: Separation and Sex

Attack #1 Separation from Dad
Where's Dad? I Need to Talk to Him

In the fifth grade, there was a boy in my class named Sidney Hadley. Back then, other than God and our parents, we all feared Sidney. At twelve years of age, he was a local boxing legend at the Kronk Boxing gym in the neighborhood—the same gym that produced boxing champions Thomas "The Hit Man" Hearns and Hilmer Kenty. On top of that, he had at least twenty-five brothers and sisters (at least that's what it seemed like to me).

For some reason, Sidney would pick on me every day and some days while in the lunchroom, he would come and take my desert. One day, he decided that it was now time for me to begin bringing him money. So he came to me with a group of boys that doubled as a cheering squad and a goon squad. He says to me, "Carlos, tomorrow I want you to bring me twenty dollars from your mother's purse, or else!"

For me, that was the last straw! I maybe would have

allowed him to take my lunch, but there was something terribly wrong with me taking money from my mom. So when I got home from school, the first thing that came to my mind was, "Where's Dad? I need to talk to him."

Today an entire society and generation of boys is asking that same question: "Where's dad? I need to talk to him."

Clearly, one of the biggest battles our boys face is the disappearance of positive male advice and input in their lives. Removing males from our midst is nothing new; evil men have done this since the beginning of time. Herod attempted this strategy in an effort to kill the baby Jesus. Witness of the Armenian Genocide of 1915-1917, the U.S. Ambassador to Turkey, Henry Morgenthau, provided one of the most gut-wrenching descriptions of *The Murder of a Nation* in a report to his superiors, published after the war.

> In it he said, "Throughout the Turkish Empire a systematic attempt was made to kill all able-bodied men, not only for the purpose of removing all males who might propagate a new generation of Armenian men, but for the purpose of rendering the weaker part of the population an easy prey."

In 1712, Willie Lynch created an entire system of breeding, beating, and separating male slaves from their families in order to reduce revolts and control them.

You would think that today we would have learned our

lesson and come to the understanding that men and boys, or father and son relationships are precious and important not only to the survival of our country, but also to the assurance that we will have future men. Therefore, any system that changes, challenges, and removes men from our boys should be quickly rejected and put down. Whether it is intentional or not, if the end result is men being separated from our sons, let's agree for the greater good that we need to stop it!

If we had the mindset of "good boys need good men," several recent separation attacks (intentional or not) on our boys would have been defeated. These attacks alone may not seem like much, but the accumulative effect is millions of boys left with no man to guide them or show them the way to the promised land called "Manhood." This leaves our sons to lean on other boys, older men who are still boys themselves, and women to lead the way.

Separation by Divorce

One such attack that separates our boys from being exposed to and trained by good men is *divorce*. According to the National Fatherhood Institute, there are over 24 million children growing up without their biological father today! In the African American community alone, of the 5.6 million black boys, over 50% of them live without fathers in the home.

Anyone who advocates or causes a divorce has participated

in an attack on a boy! God is so serious about divorce in Malachi 2:16: " 'I hate divorce,' says the Lord God of Israel, 'and I hate a man's covering himself with violence as well as with his garment,' says the Lord Almighty. So guard yourself in your spirit, and do not break faith." Wow! What if as a society we looked at divorces this way—that it was an act of violence? Here are just some of the effects of the violence on children that we were being warned about:

> Anyone who advocates or causes a divorce has participated in an attack on a boy!

Identity Confusion

Elementary-aged children are more realistic than preschoolers about the reasons for their parents' divorce and the likelihood that they will reunite. They are likely to experience confusion about themselves, because in most cases they have not yet learned to view themselves as distinct from their parents. If Mommy or Daddy is leaving, it's very much as if a crucial part of them has been amputated without explanation and without a visible scar.

Fears

Elementary-aged children are likely to be fearful about the future. They are more prone to depression than children at other ages. They are likely to experience sadness or anger, and they are more likely to be ashamed that their parents are going through divorce.

School

This is a period during which children are developing basic proficiencies on which they will call for the rest of their lives—skills like learning to spell, learning to multiply and divide, and learning how to read for comprehension. As for all children, there's a risk that grades will drop during divorce.

Anger with Parents

Elementary-aged children, perhaps because of the feelings of shame and embarrassment they experience, are likely to be angry or frustrated, sometimes indignant, with their parents about the divorce. They are more likely to demand an explanation for the divorce, and they are more likely to want to know whose "fault" it is.

Finally, although divorce is an attack against the whole family, since the fathers are generally the ones to leave the presence of the home, it surely is an attack against our boys!

Elementary-aged boys, particularly ages 9–12, are predominantly vulnerable during their parents' divorce, and especially unable to express the turmoil they're experiencing. As a result, they're more likely than most children to "act out" their feelings of anger and anxiety by getting in fights, ignoring personal hygiene, ignoring schoolwork, and engaging in other rebellious behaviors.

After the dust clears, Daddy's daughter may be hurt, but she won't have to look far for a female who can give advice, a female role model; but what about Daddy's little boy who is separated from Daddy? Who does he turn to when he needs a manhood answer? Who does he turn to when he needs an answer to, "What should I do now that Sidney who has been taking my lunch wants me to steal money from home?" Does he talk to his mom, auntie, sister or granny?

Separation by Desertion

It's one thing to have your dad walk out or leave the house through divorce. At least you have a memory of the time he was there, and there is a greater chance that he will stay in your life. It is quite another to never have had your dad live with you at all, or worst—never have known him!

One summer during a leadership workshop for teen girls, one of the students proudly raised her hand and said, "Mr. Johnson, did you know that all of us here are pregnant or already have children?" With surprise and a new sense of urgency on my face I said, "No, I did not know. Tell me how that has changed your life." Then, they taught me a few things.

The following is data from a Census Bureau survey. The Census survey indicates that in the early 1990s, most young women in the United States conceived their first child out of wedlock, a rate that has nearly tripled since the 1930s when children were born into families—a mom and dad. This number is so amazing, I came up with a new name for a birth outside of marriage. Instead of saying, "The child was born out of wedlock," I say, "The child was born into wed-not."

The proportion of children born out of wedlock, or what I call born into "wed-not," among women aged 15 to 29 grew from 18% in the period between 1930–1934 to 53% between 1990–1994, the report said. This means that today, half of children born to women 15–29 will have no father to go home to. Worst, we have no idea of how many children will never meet their father.

One reason for the rapid growth of children born into "wed-not" is that having children outside of marriage is more socially acceptable today than in the 1930s. Remember the days when we would ask what happened to Lucy? And the answer would be that she moved down South? We all knew that they meant something went wrong and Lucy was sent away.

In addition, more women are postponing marriage to pursue career goals or attain higher education, while remaining sexually active—leading to more boys being born without a daddy at home, and without a daddy having any obligation to his son.

The Census Bureau survey reported that 89% of births to teenagers occurred before marriage in the early 1990s, compared with less than 30% 60 years ago. Our parents knew better and they did not have the choice to be as irresponsible or free with having children.

For black women, the percentage of first births either born or conceived before first marriage doubled from 43% in the 1930s to 86% in the 1990s. In addition, rates of marriage before first births among black women declined.

> Sons are a heritage from the Lord, children a reward from him. Like arrows in the hands of a warrior, are sons born in one's youth. Blessed is the man whose quiver is full of them (Psalm 127:3–5).

The study also suggested that not only are women less likely to marry when pregnant in "wed-not," they are also less likely to marry even after the birth of their child. Therefore, a boy is doomed to searching for manhood by himself without the man who birthed him! Fathering a boy and leaving is like taking your son to the nearest park and putting him out of the car—something we used to do to the dogs we did not want anymore.

I wonder, if we knew how our children are so important,

powerful, and necessary to our happiness, would we continue to walk away from our sons?

Sons are a heritage from the Lord, children a reward from him. Like arrows in the hands of a warrior, are sons born in one's youth. Blessed is the man whose quiver is full of them (Psalm 127:3–5).

Separation by Distraction
Can I borrow twenty-five dollars?

A man came home from work late, tired, and irritated, to find his five-year-old son waiting for him at the door.

Daddy, may I ask you a question?

Yeah sure, what is it? replied the man.

Daddy, how much do you make an hour?

That's none of your business. Why do you ask such a thing? the man said angrily.

I just want to know. Please tell me, how much do you make an hour?

If you must know, I make fifty dollars an hour.

Oh, the little boy replied with his head down. *Daddy, may I please borrow twenty-five dollars?*

The father was furious. *If the only reason you asked that is so you can borrow some money to buy a silly toy or some other nonsense, then you march yourself straight to your room and go to bed. Think about why you are being so selfish. I don't work hard every day for such childish frivolities.*

The little boy quietly went to his room and shut the door

The man sat down and started to get even angrier about the little boy's questions. *How dare he ask such questions only to get some money?* After about an hour or so, the man had calmed down , and started to think: *Maybe there was something he really needed to buy with that twenty-five dollars. He really didn't ask for money very often.*

The man went to the door of the little boy's room and opened the door. *Are you asleep, son?* He asked.

No daddy, I'm awake, replied the boy.

I've been thinking, maybe I was too hard on you earlier, said the man. *It's been a long day and I took out my aggravation on you. Here's the twenty-five dollars you asked for.*

The little boy sat straight up, smiling. *Oh, thank you daddy!* He yelled. Then, reaching under his pillow he pulled out some crumpled up bills. The man saw that the boy already had money, started to get angry again.

The little boy slowly counted out his money, and then looked up at his father. *Why do you want more money if you already have some?* the father grumbled.

Because I didn't have enough, but now I do, the little boy replied. *Daddy, I have fifty dollars now. Can I buy an hour of your time? Please come home early tomorrow. I would like to have dinner with you.*

While researching the material for this book, I mentioned my findings to my good friend and great "thinker," Derek Sanders. I began to talk about the effects of divorce and desertion on boys. Then, feeling my work was complete, I gave Derek all the good data from my research. He looked at it, and then asked, "What about the boys who grow up with their fathers in the home—fathers who *live* there but never spent time with their sons?"

There was silence for what seemed an eternity, for I never thought of that. I asked what he meant, and he proceeded to tell me things about his childhood that I did not know. Like his dad, although he never divorced his mom, worked in the Rouge Steel plant for forty years. It was his dad's one and only job. He provided for his family but was never at home, never at church, never at ball games, track meets, or award ceremonies.

> In a small way, Derek had no father at home with him because so much of the time, his dad was dedicated to work

In a small way, Derek had no father at home with him because so much of the time, his dad was distracted by his dedication to work.

Wow! How many times does this happen to boys in our overworked and over ambitious society? Immediately after hearing his story, I began to think about the hours I put into preparing for a parent talk, training, or sermon…the hours I put into traveling to conventions and playing golf. *Maybe*

I am so distracted that I am spending inadequate time with my son. Maybe I am guilty of being physically present but emotionally absent.

My pastor, Christopher Brooks, has a saying; "It does a man no good to be a public success if he is a private failure." Well, it does a man no good to be on TV if he has no time to watch TV with his son.

Shortly after that conversation, I was watching the induction of the Dallas Cowboys receiver, Michael Irving, into the NFL Hall of Fame. With tears running down his face, he did not speak about his NFL records or passion of the game, all he could talk about was missing his son's life while he was playing.

When we were an agriculture society and men made their livings by planting, harvesting, and selling their crops, sons worked alongside their dads. What conversations and relationships between fathers and sons must have been formed then! What skills sons must have learned directly from their fathers while in the fields!

Today, many of us adult sons have been taught how to fix and repair like our dads. If something breaks around my house, I can fix it—once I find the Yellow Pages and my favorite tool: my checkbook. Like Derek, my dad also worked crazy hours in the factory to provide—and a good provider he was, but he had little time to see me wrestle or run track and cross-country races on the weekends. What would my relationship be like—what more about manhood would I know if my dad and I had not been separated? Would I have made some of the mistakes if he were there? To my brothers who are overly distracted by their dedication to careers, if you are listening, I leave you to ponder these words of wisdom, again from Pastor Brooks: "It does a man no good to be a public success if he is a private failure!"

Attack on Boys # 2—Sex: Unisex, Homosexuality, and Hyper-Sexuality

Unisex

On the way to manhood, if a boy survives the attack of separation from his father from dedication, divorce, or desertion, we must still protect him from the next barrage of attacks, which are just as deadly. In the late 60s and early 70s, the feminist movement told the nation that there was no difference in the sexes; males and females, outside of the physical, were all one sex— unisex. On the surface, some may ask what the problem is with that. Men have dominated for too long because they think that they are the stronger sex. The feminist movement has affected many changes in Western society, including women's

> The Unisex movement did not just address equal treatment for women, it caused a major change in the way we raised our boys.

suffrage; broad employment for women at more equitable wages (equal pay for equal work); the right to initiate divorce proceedings and "no fault" divorce; the right of women to make individual decisions regarding pregnancy, including obtaining contraceptives and safe abortions; and many others.

What we can all agree on is that before this movement, men were more likely to take advantage of women and women were not being celebrated for their contributions to society. The Unisex initiative did not just address equal treatment for women, the movement took an evil turn when its philosophies caused a major change in the way we raised our boys. It ignited a concentrated effort in this nation to de-emphasize the difference between the sexes, thus causing severe strain on the family unit. The answer is not to blur or destroy male and female differences; rather, we must endeavor to understand them and play to our male and female strengths.

In recent history, the most powerful proponent of feminism is Gloria Steinem, the founder of *Ms. Magazine*. Once, when asked about child-rearing, her response was:

We have a lot of people in the country who have had the courage to raise their daughters more like our sons. Which is great because it means they're equal…but there are many fewer people who had the courage to raise their sons more like their daughters. And that's what needs to be done.[1]

Based on her theories and help from many famous and influential people such a Mr. Phil Donahue and his wife Marlo Thomas, many parents began to question what real manhood was. We began to question and rethink trusted traditional roles and responsibilities such as: boys should do the hard work and heavy lifting, and our girls, not our boys, play with dolls. We also challenged the aggressiveness of our boys. We asked, "Is it a boy thing or just him being a bad boy and making bad choices?" and "Why can't boys have long hair?"

In a 1973 sermon to his Indiana church, Pastor Jack Hyles said, "One of the great signs of the end time is the fact that the unisex movement is sweeping this country. Dr. Joyce Brothers said, 'The melting together of the sexes is upon us.' "[2]

So God created man in his own image, in the image of God he created him; male and female he created them (Genesis 1:27).

God has already given us His say on the issues of unisex, gender blurring, and gender nullification. Genesis 1:27 reads, "So God created man in his own image, in the image of God he created him; male and female he created them." The following image shows how God sees the sexes.

God's way:

Unisex way:

There is a distinction between the sexes, and those differences can't be covered up or dismissed by unisex clothing and unisex beauty salons. The differences are what make male and female the compliments of each other.

The lesson we all need to learn concerning the importance of our differences can be found in 1 Corinthians 12:21–26:

The eye cannot say to the hand, "I don't need you!" And the head cannot say to the feet, "I don't need you!" On the contrary, those parts of the body that seem to be weaker are indispensable, and the parts that we think are less honorable we treat with special honor. And the parts that are unpresentable are treated with special modesty, while our presentable parts need no special treatment. But God has combined the members of the body and has given greater honor to the parts that lacked it, so that there should be no division in the body, but that its parts should have equal concern for each other. If one part suffers, every part suffers with it; if one part is honored, every part rejoices with it.

Also, science has proven this distinction with the discovery of technology that allows us to scan the brain to see how males and females are uniquely wired and hardwired, along with major breakthroughs in hormonal therapy. However, those parents that continue on the unisex path and deprive their sons of authentic manhood training will continue to confuse, delay, if not destroy our boys' journeys to manhood.

Riddle me this, if parents have the *courage to raise their sons more like their daughters* per the prescription of the feminist movement, when that son has a boy, does he raise his to be more like his sister also? And if that father and more fathers achieved that goal, how many generations would it take before society forgets how to raise a boy to be a man?

Lastly, if the boy who was raised like his sister ran into an authentic man, what would the relationship be like, and on what common ground would it stand?

Homosexuality

If our boys can be de-gendered or feminized, then homosexuality is not a big experiential leap away. In case you are wondering if the homosexual lifestyle is simply another alternative to manhood, the following information from leading authorities may help.

In 2004, the American College of Pediatricians stated the following:

Children reared in homosexual households are more likely to experience sexual confusion, practice homosexual behavior, and engage in sexual experimentation. Adolescents and young adults who adopt the homosexual lifestyle, like their adult counterparts, are at increased risk of mental health problems, including major depression, anxiety disorder; conduct disorder, substance dependence, and especially suicidal ideation and suicide attempts...[3]

The research literature on childrearing by homosexual parents is limited. The environment in which children are reared is absolutely critical to their development. Given the current body of research, the American College of Pediatricians believes it is inappropriate, potentially hazardous to children, and dangerously irresponsible to change the age-old prohibition on homosexual parenting, whether by adoption, foster care, or by reproductive manipulation. This position is rooted in the best available science.

If our boys can be convinced by friends or family not to embrace their manly difference, then what difference does it make to pursue being a man?

Homosexual activists attempt to portray their lifestyle as normal and healthy, and insist that homosexual relationships are the equivalent in every way to their heterosexual counterparts. Hollywood and the media relentlessly propagate the image of the fit, healthy, and well adjusted homosexual.

The reality is quite opposite to this caricature, which was recently conceded by the homosexual newspaper, *New York Blade News:*

Reports at a national conference about sexually transmitted diseases indicate that gay men are in the highest risk group for several of the most serious diseases. . . Scientists believe that the increased number of sexually transmitted disease (STD) cases is the result of an increase in risky sexual practices by a growing number of gay men who believe HIV is no longer a life-threatening illness.[4]

This attack on our boys goes far beyond the safety and well being of boys; the homosexual attack is an attack on women and family also. For no two men can produce another.

Then the homosexuals told us that we could choose our sex or maybe we were born attracted to the same sex. And if our boys do not fall prey to those two, we allow them to be oversexed by today's media telling them that they need sex 24/7.

Hyper-Sexuality

"A minute on the lips, a lifetime on the hips" is what is said about certain foods when dieting. "A minute on the mind and they will desire it all the time" is what is said about the effectiveness of sex in marketing ads.

The advertisement of sex, sex, and more sex is all you see in today's society. Now before you think I am going to blame the media for our kids having sex, I am not. I know that if you stranded a boy and a girl on a deserted island and returned in five years, you would probably find three people and not just two. We are programmed to procreate and there is only one natural way to do that—have sex. However, the issue is having sex at the appropriate time, in the appropriate place, and with the appropriate person. Our sons today have been overexposed to ads, cartoons, games, commercials, and songs with only one message: "Just Do It!" Our sons have been exposed to inappropriate sex so much and so often that having a female who is only a friend is almost unthinkable. There visual representations of manhood are so clearly wrong, but they are so clear. The images show that a man who has the women has the power, and he who has the power gets the women. It is a vicious attack cycle for the male psyche.

CHAPTER 4

Do You Even Know Me?

I am terrible at telling jokes, but I will give this one a try. Maybe you have heard the joke and remember how you laughed the first time. Here it goes.

Two sisters were in the kitchen preparing to cook a roast and one sister turned to the other and said, "Why do we cut the back end of the roast off?" The older sister said, "I don't know, this is how Mom taught us. Let's call her and see if there is some special reason.

So they called their mother and asked the question, "Mom, why did you teach us to cut the back of the roast off before we put it into the pan?"

Mom replied, "That's the way my mother cooked her roast. Let's call her and see."

So they called and asked the question, "Granny, why did you cut the back of the roast off before putting it into the pan?"

Granny thought about it and said, "Back then, we only had one size of pan, so we had to cut the roast in order for it to fit!"

Okay, you can stop laughing. The moral of the story is, be careful that your actions and techniques are not merely based on tradition. Many of us are parenting a certain way, for good or bad, just because that is the way Granny did it, even though today there are new and better parenting tools and information.

The proof of this is, if you spend time with youth and gain their trust, one of the biggest complaints they have is that no one knows what they are going through. Everyone assumes that many things are just like it was in their generation, or much, much worse. Everyone assumes they understand what is going on just because they were young once. They assume in the youth's world, money buys the same, school is the same, teachers are the same, choices are the same, and pressure is the same. What makes it worst is that most parents don't even know how children develop and grow. Because of adult ignorance of how children, specifically boys, mature and change, many over compensate in some areas and are too passive in others; then, by the time they catch up, their sons have changed again.

It is important for parents, or those responsible for participating in the process of raising children, to have a basic understanding of how children develop and the stages they go through. In my workshops and seminars, we often use K.I.D.

1) **K**now how children develop 2) Know your child **I**ntimately and 3) Know how boys **D**evelop differently.

Knowledge of How Children Develop

Let's start with the "K" in our K.I.D. training—Possessing
Knowledge of how children develop. In the ground breaking,
industry shaking, breathtaking thirty-year study entitled,
The New York Longitudinal Study, Stella Chess, M.D. and
Alexander Thomas, M.D. offer parents accurate information
based on solid scientific research in the field of child
development—information we all can use to bear good fruit
as we care for our children. In their book, *Know Your Child,*
which is based on the study, they present three major themes:

1. ***Babies are human from the start.*** Infants are born
    with a biological ability that immediately enables them
    to enter into a social relationship with their parents
    and to begin actively learning about the world around
    them. Therefore, from the first moment of being
    held, your child is tuning into you and into his or her
    surroundings. From moment one, without speaking
    a lick of English, our children begin listening to us
    (cherish it while you have their undivided attention).
    That also means from moment one, our children are
    effected by gunfire, smoke, and yelling.

2. ***Babies are different from the start.*** Which is to
    say each baby has his or her own temperament.
    Psychologically, temperament is the innate aspect of

an individual's personality, such as introversion or extroversion. Temperament is defined as that part of the personality which is genetically based. Along with character, and those aspects acquired through learning, the two together are said to constitute personality. The child's temperament influences his or her responses to the parents' caregiving, as well as influencing the parents' own attitudes and behavior toward the child. This explains how we can have multiple children, even twins, but have different levels or types of love and relationships with each one. We've all heard a parent testify, "One child was a darling when he was an infant, slept through the night and was always smiles, but this last one was a major challenge! That's it for me!" In this case, it was not that one child was an angel and the other a demon; it was just two different temperaments.

3. **There are many different ways to be a good parent.** Just as children have their individual characteristics, so do parents. No single magical recipe is best for all children. Chess and Thomas say, "What is critical for a child's healthy development is what is called 'goodness of fit'—that is, a good match between the parents' attitude and expectations and the individual child's temperament and other characteristics." Although that's a mouthful, what they are attempting

to get across to us is the healthy development of a child has just as much to do with the parent-child relationship as it does with the parent's parenting skills.

Now before anyone gets too happy, this study is not saying that since there are different ways to be a "good parent," there are no minimal standards or requirements that we all must meet—heavens no. At bare minimum, any parent who wants to be considered a "good parent" must feed, clothe, provide for, and protect his or her child. More to the heart of the matter is: if we want our children to fully develop, we must consider the effects of our interpersonal relationships with our children. We must consider not just what we do for them, but what we do *to* them. In truth, a "good parent" considers how his or her unique personality works to build the child into a full functioning adult.

Ages and Stages

Our children must pass through several stages, or take specific steps, on the road to becoming adults. Although there are no exact times for entering and exiting different stages, let's agree that an eight-year-old boy should be walking and out of his diapers. Experts agree for most people, there are four or five such stages of growth in which children learn certain things:

Stage 1) *Infancy*—birth to 1 year—Babies experience rapid physical growth and development. Their weight usually doubles by five or six months of age, and triples by their first birthday. Infants' nervous systems—brain, spinal cord, and nerves—also develop, allowing them better control of their heads and limbs, which enables them to explore their new environment and interact with others.

Stage 2) *Early childhood*—1 to 4 years—Huge changes take place during this stage, as tiny, dependent infants transform into children who can walk, talk, and begin formal learning. By their fourth birthday, most children attain a height that is double their length at birth. They also gain muscle control, balance, and eye-hand coordination, which enable them to become more physically active and independent. Motor skills generally achieved during early childhood development include the ability to walk, run, kick and throw a ball overhead as well as pedal a tricycle. By four, children can also eat, dress, and undress without assistance. Children also experience huge developmental changes in their cognitive and language abilities during these years.

Stage 3) *Middle childhood*—5 to 10 years—During these years, children are more independent and physically active than they were during early childhood. In children of this age group, there are significant differences in physical appearance, including: height, weight, and build. This is because heredity, nutrition, normal developmental variation, and physical activity can all affect the rate at which children grow and develop throughout middle childhood. Muscular strength, hand-eye coordination, and stamina continue to progress rapidly, allowing older children the ability to perform increasingly complex tasks, such as: riding a bicycle, dancing, and playing sports or musical instruments.

And now the moment you've been waiting for all your parenting life…

Stage 4) *Adolescence*—11 to 21 years—marks a child's transition to young adulthood. It is generally a time of self-discovery in which young people aim to define their place in the world. During adolescent development, children complete puberty and physical growth. They also develop important social, emotional, and intellectual skills, while striving toward independence and autonomy. Adolescence can be a challenging time for teenagers as well as their families. In the quest for independence, many adolescents start questioning parental authority and often show signs of rebelliousness, which can create family tension.

Teenagers also typically struggle with an increasing need to belong in society. As a result, many spend more time with friends than family. This allows teens to develop and practice social skills. However, it is also within this setting that adolescents may face issues regarding peer pressure, sexual intercourse, and experimentation with alcohol and drugs. For some adolescents, these common trials can be aggravated by ongoing factors such as: a dysfunctional family, inadequate education, and living in poverty and/or high-crime neighborhoods. Feelings of stress, confusion, and depression from circumstances related to family, academic and social life can overwhelm many young people. This sometimes can put adolescents at risk for dropping out of school, running away from home, joining gangs, developing substance abuse or dependence, having unprotected sex, committing suicide, and other types of self-destructive behaviors.

However, many studies prove that positive family relationships are a strong protective factor against these health risks and others, including sexually transmitted diseases, teenage pregnancy, and obesity.

Family support and guidance can be an effective medium for promoting values, academic success, and self-confidence in adolescents. Therefore, it is crucial that parents and other care-giving adults stay involved in the adolescent's life.

Regardless of the look on his face and the dragging of

his feet, he wants his mommy and daddy. Turns out spending time with family was the top answer to an extensive survey of more than 100 questions asked of 1,280 people ages 13–24 conducted by The Associated Press and MTV on the nature of happiness among America's young people. In second place, the next answer was spending time with friends, followed by spending time with a significant other. And even better for parents: nearly three-quarters of young people say their relationship with their parents makes them happy.

Intimacy with your child

The "I" in K.I.D. stands for *intimacy*. If you are as old as me, you remember the drama series with comedians Bill Cosby and Robert Culp called *I Spy*. There was one episode in which a nuclear scientist's son ran away from home and stole the plans to a new bomb that he developed for the U.S. Well, the *I Spy* team was called in to find him and return the plans and the boy to his father. In the opening scene, Bill and Robert arrive at the home of the scientist to get information on his son.

They begin by asking the usual questions that should be asked such as, "Describe your son. Who are his friends? What does he like to do and eat? What was he wearing?" As the questioning went on, the father became more and more agitated because it was obvious that not only did he not know where his son was, but **he did not know his son**! His son ran away and took the nuclear plans because, to him, it seemed like that was all his dad cared about. As the two detectives entered the boy's room looking for clues, they saw all the trappings of success and splendor the father had made available to his son. However, what the intelligent scientist and the father did not see was that all the boy wanted was time with his dad—time to get to know his dad, and time for his dad to know him.

A scene like this is played out in many of our homes because who has time to get to know our children intimately—know their individual temperaments, likes, and dislikes? Some who are from the "old school" of parenting might say, "That ain't my job as a parent. My dad did not talk to me, and I turned out okay. As long as I feed, clothe, and protect, I consider it a job well done."

The problem with that line of thinking is we no longer live in a society that protects its children at all costs. If we did, child pornography, child kidnapping and slavery, sale of alcohol to teenagers, R-rated movies, "Girls-Gone Wild" DVDs, soft porn music videos, gangster rap music and much, much more would be instantly punished.

It has been said that any nation that wants good citizens makes it easy to do good and difficult to do evil. Therefore, if we truly wanted the next generation of men to be and do good, we would use the power of the United States to stamp out any offender to the welfare of a child. But since we don't, parents have to be the first and last line of defense. Consequently, parents must have good-to-great relationships with their children built on trust, knowledge, the intentional transfer of values, and intimacy.

Parents today must spend enough quality time with our children with the intention of zeroing in on their temperaments, which makes up their unique personalities. Roberto Trostli, author of *Rhythms of Learning: What Waldorf Education Offers Children, Parents & Teachers,* writes:

> The primary task of a teacher is to understand the human being in body, soul, and spirit. From this understanding will grow the approach, the curriculum, and the methods of an education capable of addressing the whole child.

> This, I believe, is the secret to successful parenting as well. Parents as well as teachers who can develop a sense of understanding and deciphering temperaments will gain a deeper sense of understanding where the behaviors of the child come from. Once we understand temperaments, we may allow ourselves to move past our own expectations and really begin to see the child for who he really is.

This is not to say that a strong willed child should receive more freedom for disobedience because he was born with that temperament. Heavens no. God says in Colossians 3:20, "Children, obey your parents in **everything**, for this pleases the Lord." It does not say, "...except children with strong wills."

But when a parent understands that they have a strong willed child, they can put behaviors in context and every defiant act is not taken personally and begins World War III. Additionally, the child who is more compliant than his strong willed brother does not have to get angel's wings and a halo just to show his siblings how it is done. Parents who understand the uniqueness of each child's personality can put each child in a position to win, grading them accordingly. But when a parent does not know their child, they are left with assumptions, traditions, and "in the moment" situational decisions.

Some parents feel that just because they birthed their child and have lived with him or her, it automatically means that they know their child and their child knows them. My response to that is, geography and longevity does not equal intimacy.

In John 14:9, when Christ complained that His disciples did not know Him, he said, " 'Don't you know me, Philip, even after I have been among you such a long time? Anyone who has seen me has seen the Father. How can you say, "Show us the Father"?' "

> **"Geography and longevity does not equal intimacy."**

He was not saying they did not know *of* Him. He was specifically talking about intimacy! *Do you even know me?*

Know How Boys Develop

Finally, for the "D" in K.I.D. Now that you have some working knowledge of how children develop, let's turn our attention specifically to what boys are made of and how our sons develop. To begin this very difficult journey, I will submit to you irrefutable evidence that boys and girls are different. This evidence will come from a very popular nursery rhyme, "Sugar and Spice." It goes something like this:

> *Sugar and spice and everything nice, that's what little girls are made of.*
> *Snips, snails and puppy dog tails, that's what little boys are made of.*

Of course this rhyme is not true, but the reality of the rhyme is boys and girls are made differently. The world-renowned reporter, George F. Will, explains the difference this way: "Some parents say it is toy guns that make boys warlike. But give a boy a rubber duck and he will seize its neck like the butt of a pistol and shout, 'Bang!'"[5]

Therefore, even without degrees in child psychology or medicine, I think we can concur that since boys and girls are made differently, they will develop differently.

The question becomes: "How do boys develop?" If the truth be told and believed, there are four key forces that shape our males into men:

1. Biological
2. Mental
3. Cultural
4. Spiritual

For now, we will deal with biological force, and in later chapters we will cover the mental, cultural and spiritual development in our sons.

The Biology of Boys

Let's start with the work that goes on behind the scenes on the insides of our boys. In many homes, parents swear that one day they left their son home only to return home to a meaner, bigger, and lazier version. If you feel this way, trust me, no one stole your son and replaced him. That's him—he just has a war going on inside of him.

Our boys are biologically and unknowingly being shaped and driven by a *hormone* that outside of God Himself is one of the most powerful influences of their behavior. It is this force that pushes boys to be aggressive and risky and inspires them to win at all costs. The same stimulus turns a playful nine-year-old boy into a fourteen-year-old "Incredible Hulk." It is the hormone *testosterone!*

The study of male biology sheds light on how our sons drastically change during the teenage years when they are bathed with testosterone.

Although each boy grows at his own rate, he develops *physically* according to a well-defined plan that determines his sex, shapes his body, and influences his temperament. *Biologically*, he will unfold before our eyes no matter what we parents do. He is growing into the *physical* man that his hormones predetermine him to be.

Both boys and girls have the major sex hormones, testosterone and estrogen. Girls produce a greater level of estrogen, but boys have a greater abundance of testosterone. It has been said that a boy's being vibrates to the rhythm of testosterone!

Testosterone comes on the scene the first time in the womb when it assists in creating the sexual characteristics of the child. Then at puberty, a boy gets a second burst of testosterone in quantities *10 to 20 times more* the amount received by girls. At this time, boys have a *war* of changes going on inside of them they have no knowledge of.

They have trouble with balance, need more sleep, lose their temper easily, are moody, and struggle with concentration… not to mention the external physical changes. This all brings with it a feeling of **Power!**

It is testosterone that makes our sons feel invincible. They begin taking death-defying risks with their bodies and minds. It is a time when our boys display their programmed aggression and can become more violent; however, we must make a distinction between aggression and violence. As Michael Gurian, author of *The Wonder of Boys* puts it, "Violence is not hard-wired into boys. Violence is taught. Aggression is hard-wired." It is then that the relationship a boy has with his mom, dad, or other influential people in his life changes. If never before, this is the time that a boy needs structure, stability, assurance, and his father. This is a good time for a son to be taught Psalm 139:13–14:

> For you created my inmost being; you knit me together in my mother's womb. I praise you because I am fearfully and wonderfully made; your works are wonderful, I know that full well.

Transformed by the Renewing of Your Mind

CHAPTER 5

Media: Mood, Message, Mindset

The Devil Made Me Do It!

Ever since God made man, an external voice has been whispering in his ear attempting to persuade him to do wrong—trying to change man's mood and reprogram him with a new message so that he will have a new mindset. One that is set on evil!

That external voice is still around, with the same message and intention—death! But it is no longer slithering in a tree in the garden. The voice is coming from inside your television, from the station on your radio, and from the words on the billboard as you drive down the street.

"The devil made me do it!" are the famous words the comedian Flip Wilson used to say whenever he would get into trouble. They are also the famous words of Eve after she listened to satan. Today, any serious pursuit of how boys develop and why they behave as they do must take in account human sinful nature, today's powerful media message, and how the culture affects growth and mindset.

Today's Media

Our kids are living in a more complex media environment than we ever could have imagined when we were their age. The rules and the risks have changed radically, and many of us have been slow to grasp the difference. In the 60s and 70s, we grew up in a simpler and safer media environment. Back then there were only three major networks and PBS, a couple of key radio stations in each market, a few movie theaters, and computers were so big they filled entire rooms.

Our boys today inhabit an environment that bombards them from their first morning yawn with messages. Messages of buy this, wear that, say this, and do that. They (we) live in the most media-saturated society in the history of the world. Americans spend between ten and twelve hours a day consuming media through ever-more sophisticated technological delivery systems. The average household has three televisions and radios, two VCRs and CD players, one computer, one video game player, and a bewildering variety of newspapers, comic books, magazines, books, and other print media. We've gotten hooked on media so much that now automakers are making 24/7 non-stop, commercial-free satellite radios standard in cars.

As we enter the twenty-first century, this situation might seem to call for celebration——more media theoretically means more voices, more diversity, more channels for information, entertainment, and education. A closer look, however, reveals a more disturbing reality. Most of the stories told in our media culture—by some estimates, as much as 90 % of our media content—are ultimately owned by a handful of giant transnational corporations, including Time Warner, News Corp., Disney, Viacom, Vivendi, and Sony.

Veteran media critic George Gerbner explains that "whoever is telling the stories within a culture has enormous power to shape how people think, act, and buy. For the first time in human history," Gerbner notes, "most of the stories about people, life, and values are told not by parents, schools, churches, and others in the community who have something to tell, but by a group of distant conglomerates that have little to tell and everything to sell." [6]

> Whoever is telling the stories within a culture has enormous power to shape how people think, act, and buy.

As a result, our world has handed over much of the cultural storytelling process to a small number of large media corporations whose primary concern is not our society's health or our children's well-being, but maximizing profits. The tools of their trade are media messages and content embedded within the worlds of the Internet, video games, television, and other media gadgets. These corporations devote their energies to expensive efforts designed to mold our young people, from as early an age as possible, into brand-loyal consumers of corporately produced lifestyles, goods, and behaviors.

Spending more than 1 trillion dollars in marketing each year, big media companies and their Fortune 500 allies use media to target our children with a wide variety of products, wrapping their appeals in suggestive stories that model compulsive consumerism; push sugar, caffeine, nicotine, and other addictive products; and advertise precocious sexual, violent, and other kinds of antisocial behavior. Parents, teachers, and caregivers now find themselves on the front lines of a struggle over stories, as corporate media owners wage increasingly sophisticated advertising, branding, and marketing campaigns to win the hearts and minds of our children from ever younger ages.

How Does Media Shape Us?

Any attempt to discuss the effects of music or movies with youth today requires much, much patience and wisdom. So before you try to convince your teen that the devil is in all his music, here are some facts and understandings you must have. At its best, media is a great tool for mass education. And education provides people with the knowledge, skills, and confidence to become healthier, wealthier, and wiser. Also, education fosters a sense of compassion and mission to do good work within our communities. But that's when media is at its best.

At its best, the media is a system for mass transformation.

Why do you think we call it *television programming*? There is a very valid reason why the Word of God says in Romans 12:2, "Do not conform any longer to the pattern of this world, but be transformed by the renewing of your mind. Then you will be able to test and approve what God's will is—his good, pleasing and perfect will." What is clear in this text is that the system for transformation and conformity is found in the *renewing of your mind*. Therefore, he who controls or renews the mind controls the person!

Here's how it works with media. Music and images are processed in our brain's limbic system, the seat of our emotions. We consciously process eight frames of images per second, while our media travels much more quickly. (US television moves at the approximate rate of thirty frames per second, for example, while film travels at twenty-four frames per second.) Thus, much of our media travels too quickly for first-time reflection. According to Hunter Adams III of the New York University Department of Culture and Communication, "watching music videos accelerates the process of thinking in images rather than logic. The repetitive flashes of color and images overwhelm the visual senses and dull critical thinking." [7]

Using a VCR or DVR to slow down, repeatedly view, and actively discuss media experiences can help children make more sense out of what they're feeling. Beginning with their emotions is a useful way to open up conversations about media's power. What kinds of realities does this program build? What stories does this program tell? What are the "untold stories" here? Begin by analyzing advertisements, the lifeblood of our media culture and, per-second, the most expensive media of all. Americans daily witness as many as 3,000 ad messages, and each one makes a devastatingly simple claim: "To be, you gotta buy." Through constant repetition, advertisements work to "normalize" harmful ideas, products, and behaviors. Think of the ways in which the alcohol and tobacco industries use media—Hollywood movies, television commercials, Internet marketing—to glamorize beer and cigarette consumption.

Or take a more benign product, such as soda, which teens drink at the rate of two cans per day. Coca-Cola's charming digital polar bear campaign, which has targeted young kids for a decade now, makes drinking soda look like a family-friendly bonding experience. Mountain Dew's edgier, teen-targeted ads link consumption to a wide array of risky activities, such as heli-blading off a skyscraper. It all looks fun, but the ads don't tell us that drinking soda is linked to a whole range of unhealthy outcomes, from obesity and type two diabetes (each can of Coke contains 10 teaspoons of sugar, one of the world's cheapest substances to manufacture) to attention deficit disorders and mild addiction (courtesy of caffeine, an FDA-regulated drug) to tooth and bone decay (due to soda's displacement of more healthful drinks—water, milk, natural fruit juices—in growing bodies).

While we pay up to two dollars a pop for this unhealthy

cocktail, it costs the soda industry only pennies per can to make, allowing them to pour their tremendous profits back into huge marketing budgets, including aggressively negotiating exclusive "pouring rights" agreements with cash-strapped public schools. By teaching our young people to explore and publicize these inconvenient realities in the media stories told by the soda, alcohol, and tobacco industries, as well as other powerful marketers, we empower them to make wiser choices about their own health and wealth.

What About Music?

Not to be repetitive, but it can't be said enough that any attempt to discuss the effects of music with youth today requires the patience of Job and the Wisdom of Solomon. So let us arm ourselves with more knowledge…

First, music in and of itself is neutral, there is no such thing as an unholy musical note. Just as there is no such thing as an unholy car, bat, or gun. The life and death comes when man chooses to use something incorrectly.

For instance, one of my son's favorite shows is *Hip-Hop Harry*. It took me awhile to get used to the show because I am not a fan of hip-hop and what it represents. However, the makers of the show have found a way to utilize hip-hop's fundamental up-tempo beats and bass lines to attract children and teach them great educational concepts. Now what if I threw the proverbial baby out with the bathwater and said no to learning because it had a hip-hop beat? Sounds crazy I know, but many adults do it every day.

The International Foundation of Music Research, based at the University of Texas in San Antonio, has produced many publications on the benefits of music on early brain development. There is substantial evidence indicating that babies are aware of and respond to music and different sounds inside the womb. Hundreds of thousands of nerve cells are sprouting miraculously in an unborn baby's brain. At birth, a baby's brain development still remains incomplete. Moments after birth, a baby may turn in the direction of a voice or sound, searching for the source. A newborn quickly learns to distinguish his mother's voice from others and they are able to respond to changes in a person's voice or pitch before they reach their first birthday—mostly by moving their arms and legs or babbling and cooing. A child's brain develops its full potential when exposed to enriching experiences in early childhood. Stimuli received in early childhood are crucial to brain growth and the development of important connections made in nerve cell networks.

Music and Intelligence

It has also been proven that listening to music actually can make smarter adults of the future. Recent data from the University of Texas indicated that those students who received an arts education that included music received higher SAT scores. Many studies have shown that music can benefit cognitive abilities, particularly spatial abilities, higher reasoning and motor skills, and higher achievements in language and math. And, there's been a lot of media coverage in recent years about the Mozart Effect: the positive effect that passive listening to music of certain classical composers has on a child's intelligence.

There are certainly other intellectual benefits. For example, music has also shown to increase overall intelligence by shaping the types of attitudes, interests, and discipline within children. Many types of music can be inspiring and incredibly motivational, thereby helping children focus and improve their listening skills. Music can give children the self-confidence they need to succeed in many academic areas or in defining personality traits as they grow older.

Many researchers believe that the earlier a child is exposed to music, the more the brain responds to different music tones. We know that children are easily able to imitate musical phrases and songs. As toddlers, they love to bang on pots and pans, searching for that certain beat that they play over and over again. As they get older, they sing, improvise, move and dance, and are often introduced to instruments and formal music instruction.

In general terms, it basically confirms what we already know—as human beings, music is an inherent part of who we really are, and its exposure during a child's early years can have significant effects on their overall well-being, lasting well into adulthood. If anything, the research has made us more aware of the value of introducing our children to music while they are very young. What's most important is that we provide our children with a rich and varied environment that promotes their overall growth and development. Music can definitely play a key role in creating an enriching and stimulating environment for your child.

So What's The Problem?

Parents must also know the other side to media and music if they are to make a valid and balanced argument with teens today. If you are from Detroit and were born in the early 60s, you can really relate to my next example. If not, you should have been there, you missed some good times...

On Saturday mornings after chores, our parents would let the boys in the neighborhood catch the bus downtown to the Fox Theater to catch the double-header Karate movies. When it was all over, we could not wait to get outside and use the new moves we'd just learned. We almost wished somebody would try to rob us so we could fly through the air and dropkick him like the martial artist did. For a while, we thought we were invincible and it all came from what we saw and heard on the big screen.

Sometimes, like this example, you can see the impact of media right away. But most of the time the impact is not so immediate or obvious. It occurs slowly as children see and hear certain messages over and over, such as the following:

- ❑ Gangster rap videos
- ❑ Cigarettes and alcohol shown as cool and attractive, not unhealthy and deadly
- ❑ Sexual action with no negative results, such as disease or unintended pregnancy

According to a 2005 study conducted by the Kaiser Family Foundation, children ages 8–18 spend, on average, close to 45 hours per week watching TV, playing video games, instant messaging, and listening to music—far more time than they spend with their parents, youth ministers, or school teachers. An American Academy of Pediatrics study found that teenagers ages 12 to 14 who are exposed to entertainment media with high sexual content are twice as likely to have sex by the time they are 16 than those exposed to less sexual material.

And a study by the Center on Media and Child Health found that children who watched violent content spent less time with friends than children who watched nonviolent content. Other studies have linked music with an increased rate of drug use, and aggressive physical and verbal behavior in children.

Children learn their attitudes about violence at a very young age and these attitudes tend to last. Although TV violence has been studied the most, researchers are finding that violence in other media impacts children and teens in many of the same harmful ways:

- ❑ From media violence, children learn to behave aggressively toward others. They are taught to use violence instead of self-control to take care of problems or conflicts.
- ❑ Violence in the "media world" may make children more accepting of real-world violence and less caring toward others.
- ❑ Children who listen to a lot of violence in their music may become more fearful and look at the real world as a mean and scary place.

Although the effects of media on children might not be apparent right away, children are being negatively affected. Sometimes children may not act out violently until their teen or young-adult years. Remember this if nothing else: words evoke images, images provoke powerful emotions, emotions instantly trigger cravings, and cravings trigger behaviors.

The History and Hypocrisy of Hip-Hop

As we have seen, media, and music can be used for good or bad. Music can be used to inspire, motivate and educate. The question we all have to ask is, what is it inspiring and motivating us to do? In the youth culture, the hands-down winner and undisputed champion in music is hip-hop. No other music can do what it does, no other music has its influence and no other music has its problems.

Hip-hop started in the early 1970s in the South Bronx as an alternative to violence. Initially, hip-hop music was not violent and denounced brand mongering. When the hip-hop moguls started out, they were ignored and underestimated by mainstream companies. So hip-hop entrepreneurs started doing business for themselves and came up with names like FUBU—For Us By Us—a black fashion label. Now, that phrase could be rewritten to read Big Business Buying Us, as the biggest brands in the world tap hip-hop's youth appeal. Hip-hop has gone from fighting the power to being the power.

But the emergence of gangster rap from Los Angeles in the early 1990s hardened hip-hop, giving rise to a thug ethos that's still prevalent. An intense East Coast-West Coast rivalry left two particularly prominent hip-hop artists dead: In 1996, Los Angeles' Tupac Shakur was murdered, and less than a year later, New York's Notorious B.I.G. was gunned down in an act considered to be payback.

Now hip-hop's societal influence is so powerful you can see the gangster rappers 50 Cent and Snoop Doggy Dog in mainstream corporate commercials marketing Chrysler cars. According to Teen Research Unlimited, the total hip-hop market is worth 155 billion, and its impact is felt around the world—making it a global economic force. Gangster rap's reach is so far and deep that in any (and I mean any) community where youth can be found, you can hear rap playing. The same cannot be said about any other genre of music. When's the last time you pulled up to a light and heard urban youth playing loud country music? However, rap can be heard anywhere, in the so-called hood, the barrios and yes, even in the suburbs.

It's been said that rap is a religion and the rappers are the priests. And although that may be a stretch for some to believe, just think about what constitutes a religion. A religion is a way of life structured by common beliefs and practices. Rap negatively influences our boys' belief systems about money, women, parental relationships, clothes and how to live and die, because it is a sort of religion—a way of life. Unfortunately, this puts up a major competition with the traditional values of Christianity.

Alfred "Coach" Powell, a researcher and lecturer on hip-hop, lets us know that our boys are in deep trouble when he takes us into the world of rap with his book *Hip-Hop Hypocrisy— When Lies Sound Like The Truth*. He says there are five major hypocrisies that send mixed messages and create confusion and chaos in the hood. Hip-Hop gangsters…

1. …say they are "keeping it real" while constantly flippin' the script—i.e. changing the meaning to confuse youth perception. Example words are sex, love, murder, kill, etc.

2. …love to promote the "bling bling" lifestyle in their music, but the hood they supposedly represent is characterized by poverty and unemployment.

3. …are promoted as role models for youth even though, in reality, their rap personas and jobs as pimps, hoes, pushers, and spies serve their masters—"the powers that be" of the music industry.

4. …rap about adult themes while denying the tricks they play on youth to seduce them into the gangster lifestyle.

5. …wear the diamond-encrusted crucifix and Jesus heads and say "Thank You, God" when they win awards, but their lyrics and values promote evil themes.

He goes on to say, "Hip-hop hypocrisies are more than just immoral lies that affect one or two people; they are WMD's (weapons of mass destruction).

Why Do Our Boys Listen and Look?

Why do our boys listen, look, and follow when God has already told us the outcome? He says in Proverbs 1:10–16:

My son, if sinners entice you, do not give in to them. If they say, "Come along with us; let's lie in wait for someone's blood, let's waylay some harmless soul; let's swallow them alive, like the grave, and whole, like those who go down to the pit; we will get all sorts of valuable things and fill our houses with plunder; throw in your lot with us, and we will share a common purse"— my son, do not go along with them, do not set foot on their paths; for their feet rush into sin, they are swift to shed blood.

Most of us seriously ask, "Why?" Why do they heed the pied piper's call to sex, violence, and greed? We ask these questions because the assumption is our boys have a relationship in which they are hearing a more powerful voice of wisdom and love, so why would they choose to listen to the garbage on the radio and TV? But the truth of the matter is, we (society) have left our boys alone. We have stopped talking, training, and teaching. We have abandoned our sons to their own devices.

With almost 60% of African American children being raised in single-mother homes, who is talking to our boys? Who is telling, teaching, and training them how to relate appropriately to girls, save money or dress? With fathers who are in the home with their sons but working double shifts, who is leading the way?

While all this is going on, who do you think is doing the talking, teaching, and training? Rap videos, gangsters, pimps and playboys in the hood? Our children live in our homes, and ride in our back seats listening to their priests on headphones who shape values that are in conflict with ours and we say nothing.

Our sons listen to, look at, and follow the hip-hop pied pipers because during adolescence, hormonally speaking, they are walking risk takers filled with tension. Our sons listen, look, and follow because we (society) have stopped being their coaches on the field of life. Our sons listen, look, and follow because satan has taken time to study them, get to know them; but we (society) say, "I am busy right now…go in your room and watch TV"—***Lord help us!***

CHAPTER 6

Hip-Hop Made Him Do It

Let's go behind the mike and take a look into the art and influence of gangster hip-hop, its anti-Christian culture, and its power over the minds, dreams, and actions of our sons.

Why discuss it you ask? Like it or not, this music is not just entertainment. It is education. *Gangster* hip-hop is a school without a principal or principles, teaching lessons that you hate, being taught by teachers your son loves. It shapes our boys' beliefs in several key areas such as: how to spend money; how to dress; what to think about drugs, girls, politics, and even how to view God Himself. And as if that was not enough, hip-hop has the nerve to shape our sons' ideas of **manhood**.

> Gangster hip-hop is a school without a principal or principles, teaching lessons that you hate, by teachers your son loves.

As parents, community activists, and clergy, we need to know why our sons are so attracted to the charms of this genre.

We must know what we can do to balance the scales of power. Let's begin by clarifying some terms in order to set the stage for how the music and lyrics work on our sons.

Social Influence

Social influence affects us every day. It is the reason some believe that "—— people all look alike" and "You can catch AIDS by touching someone who has it." Social influence is the persuasion we encounter as people try to change other people's attitudes, beliefs, and behaviors. And you'll notice that the level of social influence depends on the method used.

For instance, the **compliance** method aims to produce a change in a person's behavior and is not concerned with his attitudes or beliefs. It's the "Just do it" for you must comply approach. This is the "Because I said so" method that I have to use most often with my six-year-old son after his sixty "why?" questions! (Some of you know what I mean.)

Persuasion, on the other hand, aims for a change in attitude, or "Do it because it'll make you feel good/happy/ healthy/successful." This method is the one most used in mass advertising. This method attacks or addresses your level of current contentment with whatever it is selling. The premise is, "You would be better off with our product."

The **education** method (which is called the "propaganda

method" when you don't believe in what's being taught) goes for the social-influence gold, trying to create a change in the person's beliefs, along the lines of "Do it because you know it's the right thing to do." The next time your city wants to increase taxes for their idea of better schools, think of this method.

Brainwashing is a severe form of social influence that combines all of these approaches to cause changes in someone's way of thinking without that person's consent and often against his will. Brainwashing consists of any method aimed at instilling certain attitudes and beliefs in a person—beliefs that are in conflict with the person's current beliefs and will.

During the Korean War, Korean and Chinese captors reportedly brainwashed American POWs held in prison camps. Because brainwashing is such an invasive form of influence, it requires the complete isolation and dependency of the subject, which is why you mostly hear of brainwashing occurring in prison camps or religious cults.

Therefore, for brainwashing to take its greatest effect, all that is needed is isolation and dependency. These two critical environments exist when youth in need of direction and good definitions of manhood are abandoned by good men and left alone. Isolation and dependency happen when our boys are abandoned and left to the social influence or brainwashing of the *gangster* hip-hop classrooms, its teachers, its principals, and principles and the corporations that promote it who have but one goal: profit!

When our sons are left with no man to talk to, no man to come home to, and no man to guide them through the testosterone years, they are completely isolated. Therefore, they must depend on the images they see projected as peers who obviously don't need a man to become "da" man. They must depend on the men whom they feel understand what they are going through—gangster rap/hip-hop artists.

What we must understand so that we can relay the message, is gangster rap/hip-hop is one big viral marketing scheme to deprive consumer driven youth of their money, their morality, and their minds. Their carefree gangbanging, sex escapades, drug dealing, and substance abuse should not be tolerated nor should it serve as the model for our boys as they look for a man to model.

When I am working with young men in group sessions, one of the exercises I take them through is the creation of their own "Mental Menu." These exercises request that they chart the mental food that *they* put into their minds for five days. It works because it is non-judgmental on my part, and they get to see the proof for themselves. In the music section of the "Mental Menu," I assert that the majority of gangster rap songs have the following seven ingredients:

Gangster rap ingredient I: *Death*

The song must lyrically explain how black life is so easy to take and what street offenses are worthy of death.

Gangster rap ingredient II: *The Hustler's Mentality*

The song must talk about the hunt for money at all times. Education cannot be a topic of the song unless it is street education. The song must never promote a strong work ethic.

Gangster rap ingredient III: *Lots of Sex*

The song must talk about how much sex is wanted or acquired and how good the rapper's sexual abilities are compared to other men's. Commitment and sexually transmitted diseases are not talked about unless the song is promoting how to have sex without consequences.

Gangster rap ingredient IV: *Disrespect of Black women*

African American women have to be discussed in the context of sexual pleasure, how they lie, steal, and cheat or the revenge the rapper is planning against them.

Gangster rap ingredient V: *Ghetto Life*

The songs must make ghetto life acceptable, livable, and credible. The rapper wants us all to believe that there is some honor in living, dressing, and talking within the ghetto mentality. Finally, to add insult to injury, the song wants you to believe that only a real man can survive the ghetto.

Gangster rap ingredient VI: *Drug Life*

The song must minimize the effects of drugs on our community and maximize how much pleasure, power, and profit can be made by being in the drug game.

Gangster rap ingredient VII: *Worship*

Although the rappers appear to have no boundaries they will not cross, the message of Jesus Christ on the cross is one topic they won't include in their music. If they do talk about a god, it is with no knowledge or allegiance to the one true God. The god talked about with much reverence in the music is their *money god*. Rappers have to get paid or there is no Heaven. To gangster rappers, Heaven is the place created by the god called money.

There are some who say, "I don't listen to the words, I just listen to the music." G. Craig Lewis of EX Ministries' response is:

Your subconscious records everything! You may try to block out the lyrics, but you cannot stop them from being recorded into your mind. Your mind can even record backwards messages. It has been scientifically proven that your mind is so clever that, even when you aren't trying to, you can receive the information that is stated in the lyrics of music. Even if it is recorded backwards, it affects you! When you listen to sex, sex, sex, or murder, murder, murder, those are things that will come out of you in the heat of the moment. They are programmed in your mind without your consent.

The messages in the music have gotten so bad that as I am writing, the Reverend Al Sharpton has been courageously calling on the government and radio industry to ban artists for ninety days if they have been involved in violence. In August of 2007, he led a nationwide protest called "The Decency Initiative" against hip-hop and its often vulgar and misogynistic lyrics with a "Day of Outrage." The project was taken by **Sharpton's** National Action Networks. The protests, which spanned twenty cities, took place in Detroit, New York, and Dallas. People protested the words *hoe, ni--a,* and *b--ch.*

In addition, misogyny in hip-hop music will be one of many topics explored as Congress prepares to hold its first hearing on media stereotypes and degradation of women. The hearing, entitled *From Imus to Industry: The Business of Stereotypes and Degradation,* will focus primarily on hip-hop lyrics and videos. According to *Variety,* Republican Bobby Rush, chairman of the House Subcommittee on Commerce, Trade, and Consumer Protection, said, "I want to look at not only the problem caused by misogynistic content in some hip-hop music, but also some of the pain that emanates from this degradation," adding that the inquiry is "not an anti-artist hearing, or anti-music, or…anti-youth hearing."

Then Rush adds, "I respect the First Amendment, but rights without responsibility is anarchy, and that's much of what we have now," he said. "It's time for responsible people to stand up and accept responsibility." That means you and me!

Why Do They Listen?

Many of us ask the question: "Why do they listen and why are our sons attracted to such music?" Let me suggest to you three reasons why hip-hop is so popular and powerful in our sons' lives. First, **the power of the rhythm** makes them listen. In 2006 I went on a mission trip to Uganda, and while there, I had a chance to visit with and speak to many youth at schools and churches throughout the country. While waiting to speak at a Sunday youth service filled with Ugandan teens, I remember listening to the choir and thinking, *This music has no bass, no bounce, and very little movement. It's almost monotone.* I soon discovered the church was founded by European missionaries who gave the Ugandans a bland style of music for worship.

Later, while speaking at another youth event, I heard another style of worship music where the young people used heavy bass, drum rhythms, and movement to praise the

Lord. This service was totally different and youth bounced and danced while they sang and praised. Needless to say, the energy at this service was much higher. Now some of you may now need to take a deep breath and relax—I did not go to Africa and lose my salvation. Quite the contrary, it was cemented. Nor am I saying or insinuating that one style was a better way to praise God over the other one. What was clear to me after that experience was that bass, beats, tempo, and rhythm have powerful effects on how we experience an event. Remember, the word *testosterone*? Remember the effect it has on boys when they receive a burst of it during puberty? Well what type of beat and rhythm would you imagine would be more seductive: a bland, slow and soothing beat or one filled with tense bass and drums?

This is one reason why good Christian boys can "just listen" to gangster and mainstream hip-hop, but then be drawn into the offensive lyrics. When they listen, our boys are inundated in a bath of amazing beats and hypnotic rhythms. This is why our sons listen.

Secondly, **the power of the flesh**. When you take bass lines that you can feel vibrating in your bones, amazing beats that force your head to bob and your feet to tap, and then add a hook about sex, drugs, and money, what is there not to like for an easily influenced teen? But wait—we're not finished yet. The music industry understands the lust of the flesh. They understand the desires and works of the flesh as described in Galatians 5:19–22:

Now the works of the flesh are manifest, which are these; Adultery, fornication, uncleanness, lasciviousness, Idolatry, witchcraft, hatred, variance, emulations, wrath, strife, seditions, heresies, Envyings, murders, drunkenness, revellings, and such like: of the which I tell you before, as I have also told you in time past, that they which do such things shall not inherit the kingdom of God (KJV).

And the industry wants to makes sure that our boys get as much flesh as they need; so they leave nothing to the imagination by adding soft porn to their videos. *This* is why our sons listen.

Lastly, **the power of presence**. Simply put, the rappers are there in our boys' lives and always available. What choices do our sons have? Who would you suggest our sons learn about manhood from, their overworked, unknown, insensitive, or absent father? Or maybe our testosterone-raging, hairier-by-the-day, too-uncomfortable-to-discuss-it sons should turn to Mom, Grandma or Auntie and say, "Will you show me how to become a man?" Is that your answer? God, the creator of man is an "own kind" God. He created us to reproduce our own kind, not just in species as man reproduces man, but in gender also. It is a man's job to reproduce another man.

Please don't miss this point. Moms, you are doing a great and fantastic job filling in where we men have abandoned you and it is not your fault that our boys are running to other boys to figure out manhood issues. That responsibility is ours as men, and we fell asleep on our watch. Please forgive us.

However, what mothers and fathers must know is during the adolescent years, boys seek role models and leaders...those who will show them the way on their new journey. Those who appear to have done very well and most importantly, are having fun being men. Mistakenly so, boys are deceived to believe that the boys who look like them in the videos are just like them. They believe, *If I dress like him, smoke like him, and have sex like him, I can be like him.*

As We Go, They Follow

Additionally, the filthy lyrics and lifestyles of rappers work for our boys because rappers speak for and to a generation that not only is lost but also has been left. Left behind due to our pursuits of self and stuff. As we wrap ourselves up in our nation's consumer culture and drive ourselves to attain possessions—the best cars, homes, and flat screens—our boys also get "the gotta-haves." As we over schedule our own days and become more dismissive of and distant from them—they dismiss and grow more distant from us. As we choose career over family and spend more time away from home—they desire to hang out more with friends instead of being home with family. As we walk away from relationships and marriages—they see no need in keeping any relationship in high regard. All people become dispensable to them.

All relationships are questioned and deemed "throw away" if assessed unneeded. As we seek comfort in Jack Daniels, cocaine and sex—our boys want to be comforted. This is why our sons listen!

Power of The Spoken Word:

For a long time, a lie has existed and we have told it to kids for many years. The lie got so good to us that we put it into a nursery rhyme and taught it with song. Maybe you are now singing it to your kids. The lie goes like this (sing with me if you know it): *Sticks and stones may break my bones but words will never hurt me.* Now that you are older, you know that this is a lie and words do hurt.

They hurt when someone you don't know says the wrong words. They hurt more when someone you know and love says the wrong words. But they really damage you when you don't see or understand how the words hurt. And then those same words/lyrics are put to some great music with bass and your son listens to the hurting words all day long and actually likes them! Make no mistake about it, words have power; but may I remind you their power can be used just like a gun or knife. Put a gun in the hands of a skillful, purposeful hunter and you have dinner. Put a knife in the hands of a skillful physician and you have saved a life. Put a Bible in the hands of a Spirit-filled man and sinners will come to Christ. But picture the gun, knife, and Bible in the hands of people bent on selfish motives, pure profit, or plain old evil. Now what do you see?

The same goes with words. Here's the bottom line—words can be used for good or evil. Look at how we play with words in the media. If our **enemies** drop bombs, they are **terrorists**; but if our **friends or allies** drop bombs, we call them **freedom fighters**. The Bible does not play with the power of the word. Here's how we know words have power:

In the beginning was the Word, and the Word was with God, and the Word was God (John 1:1).

He replied, "Blessed rather are those who hear the Word of God and obey it." (Luke 11:28)

So also, the tongue is a small thing, but what enormous damage it can do. A tiny spark can set a great forest on fire (James 3:5, NLT).

It is written: " 'As surely as I live,' says the Lord, 'every knee will bow before me; every tongue will confess to God.' " (Romans 14:11).

CHAPTER 7

Peer Pressure—The Wrong Rite of Passage

Today while writing at my favorite place, St. John's Golf Center, singer and teen idol Britney Spears is being blasted in all the news media due to her performance at an MTV awards event. This was supposed to be her coming out party; however, it turned out to be her take-it-off party.

The news clip showed her gyrating all around the stage as she danced with men who simulated having sex with her on stage. She performed this dance in a rhinestone bra and panty outfit. However, all the news channels chose to report was how terrible her dance routine was and how out of shape her body was—*are we that numb to public nudity?*

In addition to her pole dance routine on national TV, as if that was not enough for one night, rapper/rocker Kid Rock walked up to another entertainer and punched him smack dead in the mouth and had to be restrained. I stood there with my mouth wide open, shocked that we have come this far and saying to myself, *What pressure it must be for teens to live a wholesome and holy lifestyle today when these are their role models!* And by definition, they supposedly model acceptable roles for youth in society. What pressure it must be for our daughters to go to the mall and purchase a simple modest outfit when these types of peer examples are lifted up in front of them as models of success. What pressure it must be for them to go to their neighborhood party and not gyrate and dance with boys like Britney did.

What pressure it must be for today's girls to read, believe, and obey 1 Peter 3:3–5:

> Your beauty should not come from outward adornment, such as braided hair and the wearing of gold jewelry and fine clothes. Instead, it should be that of your inner self, the unfading beauty of a gentle and quiet spirit, which is of great worth in God's sight. For this is the way the holy women of the past who put their hope in God used to make themselves beautiful.

What pressure indeed!

The term "peer pressure" has been thrown around so much that I fear it has lost its sting. It has been used to describe everything from why we buy socks to why we go to the altar for Salvation. The truth of the matter is: peer pressure is real, alive, and very powerful in the lives of our sons.

The term *peer* describes people who are considered one's equals. *Pressure* describes the social force exerted by those peers. And when a peer uses his force to influence another's attitude, behavior and/or morals, it's called ***peer pressure***.

Making decisions on your own is hard enough, but when other people get involved and try to pressure you one way or another, it can be even harder. It's something everyone has to deal with—even adults. You don't think you bought that car, house, or outfit solely because you liked it and it fit your budget, do you? Even young children are not exempt from the pressure. Just let your son go to his first grade class where his two best friends have the *Spider Man* shoes that light up, but he has last year's *Teenage Mutant Ninja Turtles* shoes with **no lights**—*that's* peer pressure.

> When a peer uses his force to influence another's attitude, behavior, and/or morals, it's called *peer pressure.*

Positive Pressure

We have to remember also that peer pressure is not all bad. For example, positive peer pressure can be used to pressure bullies into acting better toward other kids. If enough kids get together, peers can pressure each other into doing what's right! If enough kids get together who are ambitious and working to succeed, one might feel pressured to follow suit.

As a matter of fact, a healthy part of every child's development is involvement with his or her peers. This is especially true during adolescence as teenagers develop a sense of independence from their parents.

At some point on life's journey, our sons begin to ask,

"Who am I?" The problem is they don't ask the question to *us*. This is where peer friendships can be a safe place for youth to explore their own identities. This is when peer pressure works *for* us and not *against* us. Additionally, inside these groups, kids learn about and reinforce social norms.

I remember an incident in our youth ministry study time when a few male outsiders visited us. They did not know how to, shall we say, conduct themselves around the female members. It was not long before they got the hint from the other youth that while their presence was welcomed, their behavior was not. While some never returned, a few of them returned and fell right in line with the conduct that our teens had established. The positive pressure pushed and it attracted, but what was clear is that it set a tone for what was expected.

At the same time that they are searching for an identity, our sons are searching for independence. They want and need to practice self-governance, and it is in their peer groups where they find good testing grounds. Something as simple as choosing the movie that the group will go see on the weekend is great practice. Lastly, healthy friendships provide youth with social support for dealing with some of the challenges of adolescence, such as their first heartbreak, and can also provide youth with some of the most positive experiences during those years. Many teens report having some of the happiest and most fun moments with their peers, likely due to shared interests as well close relationships.

The Wrong Rite

Because peer pressure is so powerful and because we have left our sons to fend for themselves, cultural influences, media, and friends have become the main shaping agents in our sons' lives. So much so, that the new informal rites of passage into manhood have become showing how much you can smoke, how much you can drink, how bad you can be, and how much sex you can have.

> All our boys have the potential to practice good, bad, or ugly behaviors. Because peer pressure is so powerful and because we have left our sons to fend for themselves, cultural influences and friends have become the main shaping agents in our sons' lives.

The insanity of this new rite of passage is your manhood is not determined by you surviving the onslaught, rather just being bold enough to participate does it! Maybe that's why Nike's slogan "Just do it!" is so popular, it could be the battle cry for today's informal unauthorized rite of passage.

Rites of passage programs or rituals are not just for American Boy Scouts, nor do they belong to or originate from the Jewish culture. Organized and planned rites of passage, even if they are not called by this name, exist worldwide and range from simple ceremonies, to being kidnapped by the men of the village, to body mutilation. Whatever the process, most rites have three similar phases: separation, education, and incorporation.

In the first phase, youth withdraw from the group to begin moving from one status to another in the group. This phase represents the independence and autonomy that youth seek at puberty. However, without formal structure, advice, participation, or guidance from elders, our sons are forced to follow the pied piper of popularity and the flesh. Forced to seek advice from each other. Forced to go with the flow. Truly the blind following the blind.

In the second phase, rites of passage programs re-educate or re-train youth with the skills or expectations needed for the third phase. In the *wrong rite of passage,* the values of our sons are attacked and re-shaped. This is when our boys are educated by mass media, music, movies, and magazines about such things as what a woman is and what to do to and with a woman, how to get money, and basically how to view the world. This training, although informal and unstructured, is similar and has the same effects of the training that King Nebuchadnezzar, king of Babylon, wanted for Daniel and his friends:

> Then the king ordered Ashpenaz, chief of his court officials, to bring in some of the Israelites from the royal family and the nobility—young men without any physical defect, handsome, showing aptitude

for every kind of learning, well informed, quick to understand, and qualified to serve in the king's palace. He was to teach them the language and literature of the Babylonians (Daniel 1:3).

Why language and literature? Because controlling what one reads and how one speaks—be it Babylonian, French, English, or slang, is controlling how one thinks. You see, the re-education program in Daniel's day, as well as today's *wrong rite of passage* is supposed to inform one and conform one to his new role in the group. The re-education phase is key to transformation because what the mind believes, the body follows, without question. Once the mind has it right, behavior is on auto-pilot.

In the third phase, they re-enter society, having completed the rite as a new member with greater supposed preparation and understanding of their responsibility to the group. In the *wrong rite of passage,* our sons and their friends come back to us mentally locked, loaded, and dangerous to everyone! The question is, why is the *wrong rite of passage* from peers and friends so attractive and effective?

Answer: No one wants to be alone and friends are more than friends

We adults forget sometimes how painful loneliness can be when it comes to our kids. What person would sign up for loneliness if they could be in a relationship? We forget how hard it was being the new kid or the one everybody picked on. We forget what it was like when the phone rang—how excited we were. We forget the feelings we had when the phone did *not* ring. We forget about the time when everyone was playing outside, but no one knocked on the door to ask us to join them.

To this very day, at forty-five years of age, I still remember how my entire outlook on relationships changed when, while walking into my friend's backyard, I overheard my friends saying, "Don't go get Carlos. Who wants to play with him?" Even though I had a loving father and mother at home, I wanted relationships with my friends. My peers. I wanted to fit in, and this feeling and desire is real for every kid. And for some, peer acceptance and approval is the world to them. It may not be right, but it is real and must be acknowledged and addressed. We adults can't ever forget that.

A golf buddy of mine shared with me a story of his son's battle. First, I must give you his son's resume. He was raised by both parents, speaks three languages, graduated top in his high school, and at the time of the incident, was top in his engineering class in college. To add to his educational prowess, he was a popular student, which only made any peer betrayal that much more devastating. Here's what happened. To strengthen themselves, he and a good friend decided to run for class president and treasurer. The agreement was they would win and they would share the presidency for six months each so they could both say, "I was president" on their resumes. His friend took the first six months, and you know what happened next. You're right, his friend decided he would not honor the private agreement and would not step down and their friends supported the action. This treachery devastated him and sent him into a cave filled with mediocrity, isolation, and self-pity...not willing to respond to his father's pleas. It took five years and childhood friends to come and rescue him from his emotional spin. All because of peer acceptance and betrayal.

Adults today must recognize that our kids (like us) want and need relationships with their peers. I hate to burst your bubble, but it's not enough to have your parents and talk to them. It is not enough for a son to be with his dad all day. At some point our sons need to be with other sons their age. Our prayers and practices should be to find other sons who have similar values and beliefs.

Secondly, when we don't do our parental jobs, if we are too busy, if we abandon our sons, we must acknowledge that our sons' friends become more than just friends. They become family! "My parents don't know me. Only my friends know me!" This is the statement that I so often hear and interpret from youth in ministry and in schools where I train. The magnitude of this statement is not felt until you understand how we, our sons specifically, develop.

In my day, everyone wanted to be with the so-called "in-crowd"; however, if that day did not come, you befriended those with whom you had something in common. For instance, the basketball players hung out with basketball players, swimmers with swimmers, light skinned with light skinned, and next door neighbors with next door neighbors. I think you get my point. What brought us together was a similar interest.

Today, high schools are populated by smaller groupings of friends, who navigate as a unit—the complex network of social interdependence with loyalty similar to a family's! Donald Posterski recognized this new social order years ago when he wrote:

A friendship cluster is more than just a circle of relationships. It is heart and soul of being for youth today. It is a place to belong. There is no formal membership. You are either in or you are not. Being in means you share many things: interests, experiences, intimate thoughts, problems, and triumphs of the day. Being in means you tune in to the same music, wear each other's sweaters, and generally just enjoy each other.[8]

Today, many groups of kids you see are not just friends walking home from school, or going to the movies or bowling alley. They are family. A family with a set of respected and controlled loyalties and values. If you think I am wrong, just step to a group of teens and dis (dismiss/disrespect) one of their favorite musical groups. When you do so, you don't just disagree with their music, you disagree with their family values.

A Safe Place

A standard definition of adolescence comes down to two main components—separateness and self-assertion. Around approximately thirteen years of age, uniqueness and autonomy are key. It is the period after dependence and before one can take responsibility for his or her life choices. It is also the time when adolescents begin to reflect on how they have been treated or mistreated. It is the time when they understand what the divorce was all about. It is the time when he realizes and stops caring if his dad is really coming to pick him up this weekend or not. It is the time when they see through all the political hypocrisy from adults. It is the time when they conclude no one really understands or cares for them but their friends. So the easy conclusion for youth to make is, "Therefore, my friends have to be the only truly safe place for me. Therefore, this is the group that I will follow, I will seek out for advice; and, right or wrong, this is the group that I will learn from. This is the group that will prepare me for adulthood."

CHAPTER 8

Planned Pressure—The Right Rite of Passage

Everyone Can't Be In Your Front Row

Life is like a theater, so invite your audiences carefully. Not everyone is holy enough and healthy enough to have a front row seat in our lives. There are some people in your life who need to be loved from a distance. It's amazing what you can accomplish when you let go, or at least minimize your time with draining, negative, incompatible, not-going-anywhere relationships, friendships, fellowships, and even family!!!

Observe the relationships around you. Pay attention to:

Which ones lift and which ones lean?

Which ones encourage and which ones discourage?

Which ones are on a path of growth uphill and which ones are just going downhill or just standing still?

When you leave certain people, do you feel better or feel worse?

Which ones always have drama or don't really understand, know, and appreciate you and the gift that lies within you?

The more you seek God and the things of God, the more you seek quality. The more you seek not just the hand of God but the face of God, the more you seek things that are honorable. The more you seek growth, peace of mind, love, and truth around you, the easier it will become for you to decide who gets to sit in the *front row*, and who should be moved to the *balcony* of your life.

You cannot change the people around you...but you can change the people you are around! Ask God for wisdom and discernment and choose wisely the people who sit in the front row of your life.

Remember that front row seats are for special and deserving people, and those who sit in your front row should be chosen carefully.

Everyone can't be in your FRONT ROW!!!

Because our sons want and need their friends. Because of the influence that friends and peers possess. Because it is unrealistic to believe our sons will come to us, only, or even first everytime they need good advice. Because they need us but either don't want us or don't trust us for guidance in picking friends—these are the reasons we are at odds with our sons' developmental journeys into manhood. What can we do?

One of the things we must do for our sons in this day of deception and destruction is to admit that we cannot win at this awesome task alone. How can we when they are united? How can we keep up with the ever changing fashions, websites, dances, drugs, diseases, and languages if *we* are not united? It is amazing, whenever I hear youth talk about what is going on in their life, they rarely say "I went," "I did," "I must do it again." They are always talking in the "we" form. Yet "we" adults, who are supposed to be smarter, are always talking in the "I" form. "I went to the parent meeting," "I won't let my child…," "I am going to….," "I saw…" Parents must work together in the process of protecting and molding our sons into men. If not, my "I" will never be able to keep up with their "we."

During one of my counseling sessions, a father said to me, "My son is always down the street playing video games with Mike. They stay up very late and then he is tired the next morning for school." I asked him if there were any other friends that would be better suited for their family values and we began to go through a list of boys. Finally, it turned out that another family in our church had a son his son's age. What made it even better was they lived only five blocks away and the boys went to the same school. The two fathers got together with their sons and the rest is heavenly history.

After many experiences like that, it became clear to me that if "we" and not "I" are going to win our sons to manhood, we must have a "manhood shaping" mindset and strategy. A strategy I call the *Right Rite of Passage.* We must make a preemptive strike on this culture's desire to physically, psychologically, and spiritually kill our sons. We must surround our sons with people and programs that support our values and beliefs.

The *Right Rite of Passage* People

Any manhood program able to combat the onslaught of devilous inputs that our sons receive must start with *people.* It must be well thought out, planned out, and carried out by a hand-picked group of men who have or have had sons. A group of men who possess the character of *deacons* mentioned in 1 Timothy 3:1–12:

Here is a trustworthy saying: If anyone sets his heart on being an overseer, he desires a noble task. Now the overseer must be above reproach, the husband of but one wife, temperate, self-controlled, respectable, hospitable, able to teach, not given to drunkenness, not violent but gentle, not quarrelsome, not a lover of money. He must manage his own family well and see that his children obey him with proper respect. (If anyone does not know how to manage his own family,

how can he take care of God's church?) He must not
be a recent convert, or he may become conceited and
fall under the same judgment as the devil. He must
also have a good reputation with outsiders, so that he
will not fall into disgrace and into the devil's trap.

Deacons, likewise, are to be men worthy of respect,
sincere, not indulging in much wine, and not pursuing
dishonest gain. They must keep hold of the deep truths
of the faith with a clear conscience. They must first be
tested; and then if there is nothing against them, let
them serve as deacons.

In the same way, their wives are to be women worthy
of respect, not malicious talkers but temperate and
trustworthy in everything.

A deacon must be the husband of but one wife and
must manage his children and his household well.

These are the types of men we need to identify for
molding and modeling manhood for our boys. These are the
types of men we need to use to put planned pressure on our
sons. Secondly, because our sons will often choose friends to
get advice from; because our sons will most likely dress like,
drink like, act like, and believe like their friends, doesn't it
just make sense that we use this to our advantage? Doesn't it

make sense to not *fight* their friends but indirectly or directly *help* them find and form their friendships?

As I have mentioned before, "we" is very important to youth. The power of peers cannot be overlooked or underestimated. If you study the book of Daniel chapter 1, it is clear that it was *he and his friends* who denied the king's delicacies. It was the three Hebrew boys that would not bow down. Not the one Hebrew boy! I make this point because since we know our sons will be pressured by their friends, what if they had friends who put positive pressure on them? What if your sons' friends were like the friends in the book entitled *The Pact* in which three modern day Hebrew boys make a promise and fulfill a dream to become doctors? As teenagers from a rough part of Newark, New Jersey, Sampson Davis, Rameck Hunt, and George Jenkins had nothing special going for them except loving mothers (one of whom was a drug user) and above-average intelligence. Their first stroke of luck was testing into University High, one of Newark's three magnet high schools, and their second was finding each other. They decided that they were going to bond together and pressure each other to succeed. And it worked! Wow! As you can see, the issue is not having friends, but what *type* of friends to have. Now, after you have your people in place, you need a program to place the people in.

The *Right Rite of Passage* Program

I have ridden the shoulders of my father to arrive at my today. I hold his hand as I test the strength of my legs to climb into my tomorrow.

—from an African Rite-of-Passage ceremony

If we wanted to put instructions in a bottle in order to let future generations know what to pour into their boys, what would we say?

If we wanted to help future generations prepare the next generation of men to be leaders in their homes and communities, what would we say that they must do?

If we wanted to be able to identify a "real man" from one that is impersonating a real man, how would we judge?

For thousands of years, most tribal societies have performed what we may call primitive initiation ceremonies. However, this is critical to the success of a healthy society even today. A fundamental transformation that everyone has to undergo is for a child to give up his or her childhood and become an adult.

Ancient societies always had a "rite of passage" for their young men. The entire community intentionally and methodically brought their sons into adulthood. Nature lessons were always the foundation for their teachings. Lessons for living in balance with the natural forces, paying attention to the elements, and focusing on meeting one's needs teaches a person about honor, respect, and integrity.

As mentioned earlier, most rites of passage programs or ceremonies have three similar phases: separation, education, and incorporation. Separate one from his current stage in life, educate one on his duties and the way in which he should go as an adult, and finally incorporate one back into the culture with a new view of life and responsibilities.

The *Right Rite of Passage* for our sons will have the same type of purpose. Take for instance the Jewish Bar Mitzvah. Going to a Jewish high school in a Jewish neighborhood exposed me well to the emphasis that is given to this rite. I saw first-hand how it bonded the boys together. I saw first-hand the look and attitude that my Jewish peers returned to school with. It seemed liked a boldness and fearlessness—one that I did not see in my culture. Our informal rite of passage at thirteen was to have sex, and until you had filled the peer pressure commandment of "thou shalt have sex," you were not a man.

Bar mitzvah literally means "son of the commandment." *Bar* is "son" in Aramaic, which used to be the vernacular of the Jewish people. *Mitzvah* is "commandment" in both Hebrew and Aramaic. Technically, the term refers to the child who is coming of age, and it is technically correct to refer to someone as "becoming a bar mitzvah."

Under Jewish Law, children are not obligated to observe the Ten Commandments; although, they are encouraged to do so as much as possible to learn the obligations they will have as adults. At the age of thirteen, when they are symbolically separated and educated, Jewish boys become obligated to observe the Ten Commandments and are responsible to God. This is now the age of accountability. The bar mitzvah ceremony formally marks the assumption of that obligation, along with the corresponding right to take part in leading religious services, to count in a minyan (the minimum number of people needed to perform certain parts of religious services), to form binding contracts, to testify before religious courts and to marry. Say what you want, but the Jewish people take coming into manhood seriously. My old pastor, Rev. Gregory Ingram, used to say, "Whatever a people have an interest in, they make and investment in," and if you don't know, trust me. They make an investment in a boy's bar mitzvah.

Confirmation is a somewhat less widespread coming of age ritual that usually occurs when a child is about sixteen to eighteen years old. Confirmation was originally developed by the Reform Movement, which scorned the idea that a thirteen-year-old child was an adult. They replaced bar and bat mitzvah with a confirmation ceremony. However, due to the overwhelming popularity of the bar or bat mitzvah, the Reform Movement has revived the practice.

Whatever program or course used, it should address prominent issues that impede normal adolescent development and emotional growth.

The *Right Rites of Passage* program or curriculum should contain different stages or "passages." Each passage should contain specific lessons that encompass academics, emotional growth or self-discovery exercises, and maybe even wilderness skills.

Here is one young man's testimony of how a wilderness trip changed him and his friends:

Through the world, there are many rites of passage that lead a young boy into manhood.

For many of us here in the western United Sates, those rites of passage include catching your first fish and going on your first hunt.

A few weeks ago, I had the opportunity to share such a rite with two of my young friends, Travis and Justin Osmond, sons of Merrill Osmond, as they went on their first hunt. This trip was especially gratifying for me because I also participated in their first fishing trip.

On our pheasant trip, we drove to Flowell and were guests of Don Gavin, one of the owners of Pheasant Haven. On the way down, we talked about pheasant hunting and how it was important to ignore the sound and sight of the pheasant on the rise and just watch the beak of the bird and shoot where it was going.

We got to the ranch and started hunting. Travis and Merrill spread out to the right of me, and Justin, with a shotgun he'd borrowed from his father, spread out to the left.

We started down through a row of sorghum. Halfway down a big rooster flew up in front of Merrill going straight away. Merrill couldn't see the beak, so he shot the only part he could see. As the bird fell, another came up from the right and started to go behind us. Travis got it on his first shot. The birds were collected and pictures were taken, then we continued down the field.

Not twenty steps later, another bird came up on the left. Justin fired his first shot a little behind the bird, corrected his swing, and got it with the second shot. The rest of the day went much the same. By the time we quit, our party had thirteen birds.

These two young men, Travis and Justin, had an excellent time on their first hunt. They enjoyed the time they had in the outdoors, the company they were with, and they learned new skills that will bring them enjoyment for the rest of their lives.

It was a good passage.

In no way am I saying that boys must hunt and kill before they can become men. But boys have a biological need for several hours of one-on-one contact with fathers or males each day; yet our modern culture has fathers spending surprisingly little time with their sons—little time teaching, shaping, and guiding their boys into a place of responsibility.

Hunting or camping trips provide the seclusion, survival, and co-dependency opportunities that can rarely be found at the neighborhood park. *The closest my son and I can come to survival training is when my wife leaves town for a week.* Additionally, what has been proven is: hunting teaches boys how to work together for survival. As well, it teaches them key skills needed to be providers and protectors in the real world. Whether you utilize hunting or not, any good program used should teach sons the importance of people relying on and helping each other. Additionally, each participant must master each of the program's concepts before moving to the next passage.

The following themes are addressed in many rites of passage curriculums:

- Family history
- Relationships with friends and parents
- Values and beliefs
- Independence and co-dependence
- Community value
- Family social pressures

As students progress through each passage, their level of responsibility to the whole community and self-understanding increases. At the completion of the *Right Rite of Passage* program, the community, church, and family is blessed to have the son return home. They are blessed to see him walking towards them in the parking lot. They are blessed to hear him ring the doorbell to visit. They are blessed that one more male is on his way to becoming a man.

SECTION 3

Training Our Children

CHAPTER 9

Every Boy Needs Two Fathers

> I have ridden the shoulders of my father to arrive at my today. I hold his hand as I test the strength of my legs to climb into my tomorrow.
>
> —from an African Rite-of-Passage ceremony

I will be short and to the point. I thought about writing this as part of another chapter, but it may have gotten buried in that chapter's importance and it is too important to get lost.

The best example I can give is this: what if you found a rare quarter, but you didn't want to put it with the rest of your change to decrease the chances of giving it to the store clerk, dropping it into the parking meter, or handing to your son when he hears the ice cream truck. Your other change still holds its original value; however the *rare* coin is separated to keep it from being lost. It is with this in mind that I had to put this chapter alone, for it is a stand-alone point that must be made. As a matter of fact, this chapter was not originally in the set-up of the book, but one morning while having my private Bible study time, I laid down for a quick nap before

I began my writing time. As I woke up the title *Every Boy Needs Two Fathers* was on my mind. I have learned to listen to the quiet voice inside me, especially when it is not in conflict with God's Holy Word. I certainly don't want to do an act of kindness without it having a good effect on a life. So here it goes.

In my opinion, every boy needs two fathers. If your goal is for your son to be not just a *good* man, but a *godly* man, then your son needs two fathers. If your goal is for your boy to grow into a godly man here on earth and have eternal life in Heaven, then your son needs two fathers. If your goal is for your boy to walk in blessings and to be a blessing to others, then your boy needs two fathers. He needs a heavenly father and an earthly father.

The First Father

The first father a boy needs is a father who will never, ever, ever walk away or abandon him, for He is always there wherever your son goes. A father who goes to camp with your son, a father who goes to school with your son, and a father who goes to parties with your son.

This father has not only an answer, but He always has the right answer, for He knows everything. Your son can go to Him to seek advice about all the unknowns or confusing things the world has to offer. Your son can ask, "Did man really come from apes?" or "Why do evil men win sometimes?" or "Why do I have to wait till I am married to have sex?"

Lastly, our sons need a father who has and knows how to handle power. For when our sons begin to experience their second testosterone rush, they will feel invincible. They need a father who has demonstrated how not to kill your enemies, but will say, "Pray for them." Our sons need a father who will show them how to use their strength and power to subdue and dominate with love. Our sons need a father who has power to lash out and hurt, but will choose to stay quiet and sacrifice. Our sons need this type of father, for our sons need to be able to say in times of adversity from their heart, "And my God will meet all your needs according to his glorious riches in Christ Jesus" (Philippians 4:19).

The Other Father

One of the phrases I struggle with is, "All you need is God and no one else." It is generally encouraging advice to those who are hurting from or desiring human companionship. Although, I realize when I hear it that all it is attempting to convey is God is all-sufficient and He can be closer than any brother, mother, or any other. The fact of the matter is, we are relational beings and we were made for companionship with other humans, not animals, and certainly we were not made to be alone. This is why God said, "It is not good for man to be alone," and then He created Eve, another human. If animals would do, then God could have easily put Adam asleep, took his rib, woke him up, and presented him with a puppy dog. If God Himself was all man needed, then He would have said to Adam, "All you need is me;" but He did not say it, so it must not be. We need companionship, and we need each other.

The same logic is true when people say all our sons need is God in their lives and all else will be fine. Although, as stated above, God is the number one father, He intended that boys would have a relationship with the heavenly father *and* earthly father.

Steve Farrar in his book *King Me* says it this way: "It may be hard on some fathers not to have a son, but it is much harder on a boy not to have a father."

Our heavenly father shows us the importance of the father and son relationship all throughout the New Testament. Jesus lets us know the importance of His relationship with His father in Luke 2:49: " 'Why were you searching for me?' he asked. 'Didn't you know I had to be in my Father's house?' "

Dave Simmons, who trains fathers all over the country proclaims:

Plan "A" for training family shepherds is the original, God-designed plan that calls for onsite, hands-on training in a master/apprentice relationship. It is a decentralized program with an instructor/student ratio of 1:2, 1:3, or 1:4 and takes anywhere from sixteen to twenty-two years. Fathers are supposed to equip boys to become effective family shepherds.[1]

His statement points to the heart of God's command that we be fruitful and multiply. That is, we procreate and duplicate God's family on earth. Only when fathers are intentionally walking with their son and training their sons will we *multiply* sons who grow into godly men with hearts of shepherds. Satan knows this and that is why he is so busy destroying and removing fathers from their sons lives, because he knows every boy needs his two fathers.

CHAPTER 10

Training Our Sons to *Love*

If it is desirable that children be kind, appreciative, and pleasant, those qualities should be taught and not hoped for. If we want to see honesty, truthfulness, and unselfishness in our offspring, then these characteristics should be the conscious objectives of our early instructional process.

The point is obvious: heredity does not equip a child with proper attitudes; children will learn what they are taught.

—*Dr. James Dobson, Dare to Discipline*

If we wanted to put instructions in a bottle in order to let future generations know what to pour into their boys, what would we say?

If we wanted to help future generations prepare the next generation of men to be leaders in their homes and communities, what would we say that they must do?

In the movie *John Q*, there is a scene in which Denzel

Washington is preparing to sacrifice his life so his son can live. In what is supposed to be his last talk with his son, he begins to give his son advice about what is important in life and what he must do to become a man. He gives his son nuggets of wisdom such as: he must always love his mother, and once he gives his word, he must always honor it.

If you could only teach your son three things about his manhood assignments, what would you teach him? While you're thinking, for the next two chapters I will give you my top three. Boys must be taught to *Love*, to *Leave,* and to *Lead.*

Training our Sons to *Love* Others:

It has been said that we are raising one of the meanest, coldest, and most selfish generations in history. One winter morning, I was visiting a local school to conduct a training session. As I was walking in, an elderly woman fell in front of me and a doorway filled with students. My first reaction was to try to catch her, but I was too slow. As I lifted her up and helped her gather her things, all you could hear was laughter coming from the youth in the doorway. Not one person lifted a finger to assist her…or me. Not one youth asked, "Are you okay, Miss?"

My fear is that the pains of real life, divorce, drugs, crime, and family abandonment have seriously affected our ability to do what only humans can do for humans—love. Add to that life-like dramas like *CSI*, movies like *Saw* and *Halloween*, and video games such as *Fight Night* and all the songs that glorify pain and punishment, our youth are becoming numb to human suffering. Numb to loving thy brother!

Contrary to popular belief and practice, the greatest love between two human beings is not sexual love. It is brotherly love! Real love also cares about how others wind up or wind down. And when man stops loving his fellow man, he is but an animal.

John Donne, one of the most influential poets of the Renaissance, talks about the importance of understanding that we are all connected in *Meditation XVII* from *Devotions Upon Emergent Occasions:*

> No man is an island, entire of itself; every man is a piece of the continent, a part of the main. If a clod be washed away by the sea, Europe is the less, as well as if a promontory were, as well as if a manor of thy friend's or of thine own were. Any man's death diminishes me, because I am involved in mankind; and therefore never send to know for whom the bell tolls; it tolls for thee...[9]

In the poem he says, "No man is an island unto himself," and "Any man's death diminishes me, because I am involved in mankind." Both of these statements speak to the fact that he recognizes that he must care for his fellow man and that life is more than just his personal needs.

Great American Revolutionary hero, Nathan Hale's last words are said to have been: "I regret that I have but one life to give for my country." And Mr. Rodney King who was unjustly beaten by California policemen summed it up this way, "Why can't we all just get along?" Finally, in John 15:13, Jesus says it best: "Greater love has no one than this, that he lay down his life for his friends." If laying down a life seems extreme, how about raising sons who will have hearts of good Samaritans, who help a brother who has fallen? We need sons who not only will ascend to great heights, but will also descend to low depths to help a fellow man. We need sons who will love others not because they live on the same block, are in the same fraternity, or the same skin color, but because they are from the same heavenly father, and understand that whatever affects one directly, affects all indirectly.

As Martin Luther King said in his speech to the garbage workers union:

> As long as there is poverty in the world, I can never be truly rich, even if I have a million dollars. As long as disease is rampant and millions of people in this world cannot expect to live more than twenty-eight or thirty years, I can never be truly healthy. I can never be what I ought to be until you are what you ought to be.

Training our Sons to *Love* A Woman:

Now when it comes to fleshly, sensuous, and sexual love (Eros) our sons have that mastered, and they should. Since they began watching TV, we have robbed them of their innocence by bombarding them with sexual messages—even the cartoons we feed them contain adult concepts and display the detailed body parts of women. As I am writing this page, I read a news report saying:

> After an outbreak of pregnancies among middle school girls, education officials in this city have decided to allow one school's health center to make birth control pills available to girls as young as eleven.[10]

These young ladies did not get pregnant by themselves, they had help, and the help came from our sons. Our sons need to know about what real love is and why sex is worth waiting for, no matter what they see, hear, or think.

In addition to their lustful mindsets, our sons have also been exposed to perverse definitions of love as they've seen terrible abuse of women in and out of the family setting. Rightfully so, our sons are very confused. Sometimes their very own mothers are abused for what is called *love*. One of the techniques for profiling a serial killer is discovering his love-hate relationship with his mother. Therefore, one way to stop a future serial killer is to love our sons and teach our sons how to love the right way. Our sons need to know the truth about love from us before they leave and enter the world searching for a life long mate to enter into covenant with.

> ## Loving a woman is a man's job.

A wise woman once said, "Loving a woman is a man's job."

However, if our sons are left to figure this one out for themselves, it would be similar to leaving them in the kitchen with a gas stove and matches and saying, "Light the fire, I will be back!"

If we leave match making to our sons, they will undoubtedly follow the popular method. The popular formula for choosing a mate is simple, it is 90% external (how she looks) and 10% self (what she can do for me). If our sons are left to themselves without proper training in this area, their flesh and the Jezebels will always win over the virtuous women of the world. The women described in Proverbs 31:10–30:

The Wife of Noble Character

A wife of noble character who can find?
She is worth far more than rubies.
Her husband has full confidence in her
and lacks nothing of value.
She brings him good, not harm,
all the days of her life.
She selects wool and flax
and works with eager hands.
She is like the merchant ships,
bringing her food from afar.
She gets up while it is still dark;
she provides food for her family
and portions for her servant girls.
She considers a field and buys it;
out of her earnings she plants a vineyard.
She sets about her work vigorously;
her arms are strong for her tasks.
She sees that her trading is profitable,
and her lamp does not go out at night.
In her hand she holds the distaff
and grasps the spindle with her fingers.
She opens her arms to the poor
and extends her hands to the needy.
When it snows, she has no fear for her household;
for all of them are clothed in scarlet.

She makes coverings for her bed;

she is clothed in fine linen and purple.

Her husband is respected at the city gate,

where he takes his seat among the elders of the land.

She makes linen garments and sells them,

and supplies the merchants with sashes.

She is clothed with strength and dignity;

she can laugh at the days to come.

She speaks with wisdom,

and faithful instruction is on her tongue.

She watches over the affairs of her household

and does not eat the bread of idleness.

Her children arise and call her blessed;

her husband also, and he praises her:

"Many women do noble things,

but you surpass them all."

Charm is deceptive, and beauty is fleeting;

but a woman who fears the LORD is to be praised.

This is the type of woman we should be training our sons to look for and to fall for. This is the type of woman we should want our sons to love.

After they have been taught how to love one another and love women, they are safe to go into the world. If your son can't love others or doesn't know how to love women, please keep him to yourself and save the rest of us the pain. If he has passed your class, please send him to us so we can share in your joy!

Training our Sons to *Love* God:

I intentionally saved this *love* for last; even though by all rights it is the foundational love needed in order for us to correctly and completely achieve the former discussed loves. This *love* not only provides the healthy definition for loving mankind and loving a woman, but this love is the source of power needed to complete the job. It is the source of power needed to love another brother when that brother is hard to love.

This *love* provides the man with the manpower needed to love his wife and children when life gets tough. For even though the marriage covenant says "for better or worse," sometimes the "worse" comes first. If that should happen, this *love* provides our sons with the power to suck it up and continue to have faith that he can win.

Without the power and direction of this *love,* our boys will grow up using a shallow, selfish, and self-serving love as their measuring stick to choose friends and wives. Without this power, our sons will forever have a revolving door of relationships, for should someone not bring them pleasure, they will cut them off. Without the power and direction of this *love,* our boys will continue the cycle of abandonment that plagues today's families.

The main reason this generation of boys is so narcissistic and loves others only when others love them or when times are good is, they don't fear, know, or believe in a heavenly definition of *love*. They know no love higher than oneself! Therefore, they are limited to a shallow and selfish love.

Don't get me wrong; I could not do what I do effectively without being aware of the alarming statistics of teen suicides and self-destructive behaviors. Today's sons need to have high self-esteems so they won't self-destruct. However, let's teach them to love themselves with rational, healthy, and moral self-interest. Let's also teach them to love their neighbors as themselves, but most importantly, let's teach and train them to:

> Love the Lord your God with all your heart and with all your soul and with all your mind and with all your strength (Deuteronomy 6:5).

CHAPTER 11

Training Our Sons to *Leave*

Ohne of the questions I ask parents at our "Power Paren-T-een" workshops is, "What are you training your son for?" As you might guess, the answers vary. For various reasons, many parents are in reaction mode most of the time when it comes to training. What I mean by that is, training begins because some situation caused it to. Dating training begins because the mother found condoms in the washing machine. That's reactionary training. Training your son about girls because he is male and soon will have desires and questions is *proactive* training.

One of the trainings that often goes untouched until it's too late and frustration, complacency, and laziness have set in, is training our sons that they must leave our homes. Therefore they must have the proper skill sets to live independently. In recent years, because of the emotional or financial codependency that many mothers have with their sons, many sons don't leave the household until pushed out or until they find another woman who will provide for them. One of the true signs of authentic manhood is when a man can either provide for himself or provide for his family. Sadly, due to missed preparation and misunderstood purpose, our sons today are not leaving our homes the right way or for the right purposes. Even worse, some are not leaving at all! In the series *The Cosby Show*, Cliff and Clair Huxtable often joked about the kids plotting to wait until they died to get the house. Cliff subtly infused the concept that kids are to be expected to leave the parents' home and be on their own. Although he never gave us a reason why, I agree with him 100%. God gave us one of His reasons and His command that sons leave in Matthew 19:4–6:

> And He answered and said to them, "Have you not read that He who made *them* at the beginning '*made them male and female*,' and said, '*For this reason* **a man shall leave** *his father and mother and be joined to his wife, and the two shall become one flesh*'"? So then, they are no longer two but one flesh. Therefore what God has joined together, let not man separate" (NKJV).

This says that our sons should be expected and trained to leave us and go cleave to their wives. The heavenly expectation is vital if we are to follow the commandment given to us in Genesis to "be fruitful and multiply." How will our sons be able to fulfill this if we won't let them leave our bedrooms or basements? How would they be able to survive away from us if we did not intentionally prepare them for leaving? Why would they desire to leave if they continued to get their clothes washed, food cooked, and bills paid at our addresses?

Skills Needed For *Leaving:*

The following are five of my top skills I believe every son should possess in preparation of his leaving. These skills should be intentionally taught as a part of a proactive parenting program, launching the son out into the world ready to lead a productive, independent life. They are in no particular order and without any particular age requirements. However, they should be introduced and taught at age appropriate times.

Leaving Skill #1—A Biblical World View

I am five foot six, bald headed, brown skinned, and I have a mustache, but none of this had anything to do with me—I had no say so. However, my actions primarily stem from how I think and what I believe. There is a saying that goes, *If you want to make a difference in the way people live, start by making a difference in the way people think.*

The same wisdom works for the preparation of our sons. We have to make a difference in how our sons process the onslaught of information, advertisements, and downright temptation that comes at them each day. We can't take for granted that they will think like us!

A *worldview* is the lens or grid through which we interpret the world, the universe, and every principle of what is right or wrong with all individuals, families, cultures, and nations. A biblical worldview says our sons will look at movies, listen to music, and choose friends through a lens that considers and is consistent with their belief system.

Leaving Skill #2—Critical Thinking Skills

While working with teens as much as I do, I am often amazed at what they will say and do. For instance, when a son or daughter is questioned, and the truth is discovered, it's obvious that they just did not think the issue through correctly to begin with. Personalize this by asking your son to complete a task without giving him step by step details and see if when you return it is completed. I am not talking about it being not done because he forgot or is still playing his video game. I am talking about it not being done because something was missing and he could not figure it out. I test my six-year-old son's critical thinking skills by intentionally leaving out one part to see if he will think it through. As he gets older, I will leave out more steps.

One summer while at a local high school championship basketball game, one of the player's dads turned to me and asked if I would work with his son. I said, "I am flattered but I know very little about training basketball players." He went on to explain he was not talking about basketball, but he needed help with his son's decision making *off* the court.

On the court, this kid knew exactly the right thing to do if his team was down two points with fifteen seconds left on the clock. But if his friends said, "Come on, Mary's parents are gone for the weekend and her friends have just invited us over and all we have to do is bring the beer!" he was in trouble.

A better sign of our youth not critically thinking things through is when their so-called idols consistently and blatantly lie to them on TV and in their music. Critically thinking youth would see right through their hypocrisy and selfishness. As it is today, even in the face of teenage pregnancy, STDs, and historic levels of incarcerations, our youth are locked and loaded on instinct only. The irony of it all is critical thinking is the one thing that separates us from the animals! Ask a young man why he has sagging pants, and the response will be "I don't know" or "Cause I want to." Ask him: "Can you run if you had to get away in a hurry?" or "Do you get tired of pulling your pants up all the time?" or "Why don't you like tying your shoes?"

These questions require one to think, but most don't want to—it's easier just to go along with the crowd.

Leaving Skill #3—Relationships

The old saying goes, "It's not what you know, but who you know." I would add to that cliché "...and how you get along with them." One of the tips that employers remind me of to pass on to the teens I work with is, "What you know gets you the interview and maybe even the job, but how you fit into our organization is what moves you upward."

Too many times, youth have the idea that the only people they have to obey is their parents and the only people they have to get along with are the people they *want* to get along with. That is not true in the world and it is not true from a biblical worldview. Charles Swab, an investor, was the first man in America to be paid a million dollar salary. He was paid this enormous amount by a man who, at that time, was the richest man in America—Mr. Andrew Carnegie. Mr. Carnegie said he paid that amount because no one could negotiate deals and turn disagreeable situations into win-win opportunities like Swab. "The man knew how to build good relationships," Mr. Carnegie said. "His smile alone was worth the million."

The key to becoming good at relationships is knowing how to navigate the big three: subordinate relationships, peer relationships, and superior relationships. When our sons don't know how to treat those less fortunate than them, equal to them, or in authority over them, they will be in our homes for a long time.

Luke describes Christ's relationship skills this way: "And Jesus grew in wisdom and stature, and in favor with God and men" (Luke 2:52). Even Christ Himself knew it was important to get along with His fellow man. How else could He witness to others? How could He relate to their struggles if He did not relate to them personally?

Leaving Skill #4—How to Handle Money

I saw a young mother in the supermarket recently with a toddler perched in her shopping cart and another child walking alongside the cart. Before starting down the aisles, she stopped briefly at the automated teller machine, inserted her card, punched in a few numbers and grabbed the cash as it spit out of the slot. The children were watching.

I wondered if these young children would ever learn that their mom worked a full-time job, paid taxes, and even set money aside for their college education—all before she could withdraw the cash to pay for the groceries. That evening, as I watched the ecstatic winner of a 100 million dollar lottery on the evening news report, I thought about the many children who would grow up believing that having money is a matter of street hustle, luck, and winning numbers.

In my day, my parents would say to me, "Money doesn't grow on trees." Now we have to teach them that money doesn't come from ATMs or lottery tickets or casinos. It comes from hard work and it comes with responsibility.

If indeed our sons are expected to become good and godly men who will lead and be responsible for providing for themselves and someone's daughter, then they must know how to respect money. If you believe as I do, that we are only stewards of what God has given us, then we must teach our sons how to be responsible with what is given to his care. At the very least, our sons must know how to respect and handle money so they can move out on their own and not have to call us each month for rent money.

Leaving Skill #5—Work Ethic

Thomas Edison once said, "Genius is 1% inspiration and 99% perspiration. Accordingly, a genius is often merely a talented person who has done all of his or her homework."

Timothy said, "But if anyone does not provide for his own, and especially for those of his household, he has denied the faith and is worse than an unbeliever" (1 Timothy 5:8, NKJV).

Bill Gates recently gave a speech at a high school. In the speech, he quoted from *Dumbing Down Our Kids* by Charles Sykes the eleven rules kids did not and will not learn in school about hard work. He talks about how feel-good, politically correct teachings created a generation of kids with no concept of reality and how this concept set them up for failure in the real world. Love him or hate him, he sure hits the nail on the head with this! To anyone with kids of any age, here's some advice:

Rule 1: Life is not fair—get used to it!

Rule 2: The world won't care about your self-esteem. The world will expect you to accomplish something before you feel good about yourself.

Rule 3: You will not make $60,000 a year right out of high school. You won't be a vice-president with a car phone until you earn both.

Rule 4: If you think your teacher is tough, wait till you get a boss.

Rule 5: Flipping burgers is not beneath your dignity. Your grandparents had a different word for burger flipping: they called it opportunity.

Rule 6: If you mess up, it's not your parents' fault, so don't whine about your mistakes, learn from them.

Rule 7: Before you were born, your parents weren't as boring as they are now. They got that way from paying your bills, cleaning your clothes, and listening to you talk about how cool you thought you were. So before you save the rain forest from the parasites of your parent's generation, try cleaning the closet in your own room.

Rule 8: Your school may have done away with winners and losers, but life has not. In some schools, they have abolished failing grades and they'll give you as many times as you want to get the right answer. This doesn't bear the slightest resemblance to anything in real life.

Rule 9: Life is not divided into semesters. You don't get summers off and very few employers are interested in helping you find your purpose in life. Do that on your own time.

Rule 10: Television is not real life. In real life people actually have to leave the coffee shop and go to jobs.

Rule 11: Be nice to nerds. Chances are you'll end up working for one.

Lastly, what would you say if your daughter wanted to marry a man who could not keep a job due to his laziness or would not work at all? We must teach our sons to work and work hard.

CHAPTER 12

Training Our Sons to *Lead*

Now that you have trained your son to *love* and to *leave,* he has skills which will allow him to survive independently. Now, the third training is just as important. His third training is for a greater purpose than just for himself, for if we stopped at *love* and *leave,* we could raise our sons to be selfish and self-serving. His third training makes him whole and ensures that those in his care are safe and almost ensures that you will be able to enjoy the grand-parenting years. His third training is for the benefit of starting and guiding his own family!

The third training of our sons after *loving* and *leaving* is *leading!* The command is for a man (our sons) to leave, cleave, multiply, and to be the loving head of his household. They can attempt this one of two ways. Either they can be thrown to the wolves so to speak and learn how to lead a household "on the fly" once they are married, or we as parents can be proactive and jumpstart their knowledge of leading a family before they start one.

The choice is yours; however, the "on the fly" strategy is one of the main contributors to why men marry late and leave families early when they get the shock of the responsibility and self-sacrifice it requires. This lack of strategy is one of the main reasons that instead of you enjoying being a grandparent, you have to become a fill-in parent again for your grandchildren.

Here's a novel idea: what if our sons left home with a desire for a family? Or what if our sons left home knowing that they would have to show leadership for their family, that they, and not their wives, would be held responsible for the well-being of their family?

Let's make it personal… What if your son left home willing, able, and ready (at the appropriate time) to start and lead his family? If that is your dream and plan, your son will need to know a few key leadership concepts to complete the job.

Leadership Skill #1—Being the Point Man

Before I met and married my wife Melissa, I was on a date with a young lady and we were on our way to the mall. While driving in the mall parking lot, we discussed which way JCPenney was so we could park close to the entrance. I believed it was left, she said right. For a moment in time we were paralyzed in the car as to which direction to go. She insisted I turn her way and I insisted on the other way. She believed she was right and I did too. She wanted to lead and so did I, but somebody had to lead because we were going nowhere fast. It was then I remembered a valuable teaching:

"Two heads are better than one only when both heads are heading in the same direction."

Since we were at a standstill and I wanted to impress her on our first date, I made the decision to go her way. However, it turned out that the store was the other way—the way I had suggested. The moral of the story is not that men are always right; if we were, you would not hear us fathers say, "Ask your mother." If we

> **"Two heads are better than one only when both heads are heading in the same direction."**

were always right, we men would not need the new electronic Global Positioning Systems (GPS) in our cars. For we would rather donate blood than pull over and ask for directions.

That's not my point at all; my point is Mr. Henry Ford was right by building cars with only one steering wheel because only one person can drive. Not that the passenger knows nothing and has no room to give input, but at some point some*one* has to take the wheel in his hand and lead the way.

God has assigned this leadership role and responsibility to the *man,* so he must be on point to lead his family—not because his wife is inferior, but there must be order. He must be ready to lead not because his wife is weak, but because a wise man once said, "Anything with no head is dead, and anything with two heads is a freak."[11] (If you're wondering about my date, she and I did not work out for some reason.)

In the book *Point Man,* Steve Farrar tells the story of a military Point Man:

Welcome to Vietnam....

You are going out on patrol. You've been on patrol before, but today is different. It's different because the patrol leader has appointed *you* to be "*Point Man.*" You're the leader. Everyone else will fall in behind you

You realize as you move out to encounter the enemy those behind you will depend upon just one thing: *Your Ability to Lead*

Entire patrols have been lost because the *Point Man* failed to anticipate an ambush. Men have been killed or horribly maimed, all because a *Point Man* lacked **skill and wisdom!!** [12]

This is no imaginary situation. It is reality. If you are a husband or father, then you are in a war. Leading a family through the chaos of American culture is like leading a small patrol through enemy-occupied territory. The casualties in this war are as real as the names etched on the Vietnam Memorial. The casualties are our family members. The casualties are our sons, in-laws, grandchildren and future generations. I know you are saying, "Come on Carlos, you are taking this leadership thing to seriously."

My response is no, on the contrary we are not taking it seriously enough!

> "Most sons negatively or positively affect at least four generations."

I have a four-generation philosophy which simply states "Most sons negatively or positively affect at least four generations." Let me explain. Most sons have an interacting and overlapping effect on:

1) his parents' generation
2) his own generation
3) his children's generation
4] his grandchildren's generation

I will use my dad's life as an example. **First,** my father was an abusive alcoholic. Because of his leadership, my grandparents had to spend time and money supporting his family. **Secondly,** my father's generation, friends, and neighbors were exposed to this behavior and were either repulsed by it or accepted it, but nonetheless were affected by it. **Thirdly,** I was surely affected by his leadership and it affected the way I interacted with my wife and son. Although I received much grace throughout my life, many children of alcoholics have a rough time. Just read the following information about children of alcoholics:

A child in such a family may have a variety of problems:

<u>Guilt</u>. The child may see himself or herself as the main cause of the mother's or father's drinking.

<u>Anxiety</u>. The child may worry constantly about the situation at home. He or she may fear the alcoholic parent will become sick or injured, and may also fear fights and violence between the parents.

<u>Embarrassment</u>. Parents may give the child the message that there is a terrible secret at home. The ashamed child does not invite friends home and is afraid to ask anyone for help.

<u>Inability to have close relationships</u>. Because the child has been disappointed by the drinking parent many times, he or she often does not trust others.

<u>Confusion</u>. The alcoholic parent will change suddenly from being loving to being angry, regardless of the child's behavior. A regular daily schedule, which is very important for a child, does not exist because bedtimes and mealtimes are constantly changing.

<u>Anger</u>. The child feels anger at the alcoholic parent for drinking, and may be angry at the non-alcoholic parent for lack of support and protection.

<u>Depression</u>. The child feels lonely and helpless to change the situation.

Finally, my son was affected for he has little if any relationship with his grandfather. No fishing trips, no Christmas gifts, and no wise counsel from the gray-haired old man. And even with the human and divine intervention in my life, my son has a different father because of my dad. There it is, four generations affected by the leadership of one man. Our sons must learn to be a good and godly *Point Men,* four generations depend on it.

Leadership Skill #2—Being a Partner

When I first started my business in 1991, I remember having to file corporation papers with the City of Detroit and State of Michigan. The one question that was asked on every form was what my business structure was.

They wanted to know if I was a non-profit, LLC, sole proprietor, or partnership so they could determine how I would act as a business.

If our sons are going to follow God's command to leave and cleave to their wives, we must help them answer a similar question about their family structure.

There are several models that our sons can follow. One model is the *single man* model. In this model, our sons go through life constantly interviewing female partners—never agreeing to settle with one. Most times he will be interviewing multiple partners at the same time. In this model, our sons show up each year at the family Christmas gathering with a new potential partner for everyone to meet and interview. And as long as she is pretty, no one (especially the men of the family) says anything about it. In this model, if our sons are not set aside for a good and godly work until he marries, he will find himself contributing to the future pain and disadvantages that all children go through when there is no father in the home. Or we will find ourselves taking care of our grandchildren and having a lot of unnecessary family drama added to our lives.

Our sons could also choose the *absent or abandoning man* family model. This is when a man decides that he will leave the family dwelling and live in another location. Either selfishness, a situation beyond his control, or society tells him, "You don't have to be there to be a good father." He is told it is okay to abandon the household and the kids. If our sons don't physically leave the house, they could elect to be home but be psychologically or emotionally absent.

If remaining single, abandoning, or being unreachable does not appeal to our sons, they could choose to marry and have children but have the wrong philosophy about how to interact with their children and wife. They could have the belief that the house and all that dwell in it are his to control and dominate. Our sons could choose the *dictator man* model. Plain and simple, this leader must know everything and approve everything, and if he does not, there will be a price to pay. The *dictator* rules with fear that he confuses with love; he has forgotten or does not know that perfect love casts out all fear. He does not know that there is a difference between a healthy fear and an unhealthy fear.

The leadership model we should train our sons to choose—and I pray our sons will choose it—is the *partnership* model.

This model of leadership teaches and trains our sons that their wives have value; for they are our partners not our maids or hired hands, and the success of our prayers are tied into how we treat them. 1 Peter 3:7 says it this way: "Husbands, likewise, dwell with *them* with understanding, giving honor to the wife, as to the weaker vessel, and as *being* heirs together of the grace of life, that your prayers may not be hindered" (NKJV).

> Husbands, likewise, dwell with them without understanding them, giving no or little honor to the wife, as she is the weaker vessel, and you are the superior one!

Maybe if we updated this passage with the modern day application our modern day errors will be easily magnified. Instead of following 1 Peter 3:7 correctly, this is how we operate today: *Husbands, likewise, dwell with them [your wives] without understanding them, giving no or little honor to the wife, as she is the weaker vessel, and you are the superior one!*

Leadership Skill #3—Being the Priest

Maria and Marcus came to me to seek an objective opinion about a dispute they were having over disciplining their son Mario. The issue was Mario would not eat unless the different foods on his plate did not touch. The example Marcus, his dad, gave was he did not like his mashed potatoes touching his peas so he would not eat. Marcus believed that a child should not have the choice to put those types of demands on his parents and said, "If the boy won't eat, he goes hungry, but I am not about submit to a child's demand." Maria believed that Mario, her son, had the right to make choices about the very food that he would eat.

Although this is a great opportunity to teach about a child's submission, creating healthy boundaries, and learned disobedience, I will stick to the point of our sons being priests in their homes. However, if you had this battle last night and want answers, read what Dr. James Dobson says in his bestselling book, *The Strong Willed Child,* or J. Richard Fugate's strategy in *What the Bible Says About Child Training.* The point in this story, however, is even though their disagreement seemed to revolve around food; the real issue of disagreement was each other's beliefs. The two senior heads of the house had conflicting beliefs, which caused a dispute. In this example, the conflicting beliefs were about food, but what if the conflicting beliefs were about faith? What if Maria believed that all you need do is believe in any god for they are all the same, just with different names and that Heaven is promised to you; but Marcus believed that true faith demonstrated by obedience to the one true God is the only way to Heaven? Can you imagine the spiritual trauma or at least confusion their son would have? This is why, when our sons are trained to take on the responsibility of the *Point Man,* they must include in their leadership role leading their family in faith. The priest role is to lead their family in their beliefs. This does not mean that the father must know at least one more Scripture than his wife and children in order to qualify for leadership. It means that his desire for his family to believe the truth and the same truth must be second to none. A man with a desire that great will encourage, inspire, and support the faith of his family while punishing those who come against his faith. A man like this has a greater chance of multiplying his faith in the hearts of his children and grandchildren. A man like this is the priest of his home.

Leadership Skill # 4 & 5—Protector and Provider

These last two skills I have combined for they go hand and hand, and they will be deal breakers for most of our sons' families. For if our sons cannot *protect* or *provide* for their families, their leadership position is up for grabs. Their leadership position is rightfully questioned, and frequently challenged. If our sons cannot protect or provide and accepts this status, their

> With very few exceptions, even the animal kingdom operates on this paradigm. The male protects and provides.

leadership position in their home is in jeopardy. With very few exceptions, even the animal kingdom operates on this paradigm. The male protects and provides.

While my entire house was sleeping one night, my wife and I awoke to the sound of movement downstairs or outside—we could not distinguish. I knew I dared not turn to my wife and say, "Honey, did you hear that noise? Please check it out and secure the house." I could have said it, but the rest of my life would have been miserable. As a matter of fact, it never entered in my mind. There is a reason that God created men with the muscular make up that we have, and there is a reason that we have ten to twenty times the testosterone than women do. The reason is for us to get out of bed and protect our families. The reason is for us to get out of bed and go subdue and have dominion. Our sons must know that the protection of their family is their responsibility; however, the role of protector is shared. For instance, a friend of mine shared with me his strategy for protecting his family from what he calls "garbage gadgets." He says, "The fastest growing portal for providing pornography, violence, and other anti-Christian values is our children's very own cell phones, but I can't keep up with it all by myself, so my wife has taken on the role of 'technology cop' in our home."

He adds, "We both agree that we must protect our children from the filth that comes through technology, but she is the one who stays on top of all the new gadgets and gimmicks so our son can't be tricked or so our son can't trick us. I am still responsible for protection for the family if we are attacked, but her role is to keep us updated on the attacks and the weapons we can use to fight back."

Now ever since we have left our farming communities where men plowed, planted, and harvested their own food; ever since we stopped going out as village hunting parties to kill wild game to feed our families; and more recently, ever since WWII when the men of the country were away fighting and the wives, in their absence, had to take over financial leadership of the home by going to work, the concept of the man being the sole provider has had some major updates. Add to that a new economic reality that wives can earn as much as their husbands and the man's role and responsibility to provide has to be reexamined for today's home. Nevertheless, don't be fooled by current updates to the family landscape. Our sons are still responsible for the financial provision of their families, but new opportunities for women do cause us to have to prepare our sons differently.

What if our sons marry well and their wives make more money? Are they still responsible for provision in the household? What do we do with 1 Timothy 5:8 that says, "But if anyone does not provide for his own, and especially for those of his household, he has denied the faith and is worse than an unbeliever"?

> But if anyone does not provide for his own, and especially for those of his household, he has denied the faith and is worse than an unbeliever.

What we must understand again is the distinction between *responsibility* and *role*. No matter who makes the most money, the responsibility for the family's provisions is the husband's. The key words in 1 Timothy are *does not provide*. We are talking about a man's heart, desire, and application—not dollar amount. Our sons should still provide financial wisdom, self-control, guidance, and leadership. Our sons must still get up out of bed and hunt for the family. As a matter of fact, not only should they get out and hunt, but it is their heavenly responsibility to do so. However, now his wife may be hunting also.

CHAPTER 13

Discipline: Thy Rod and Thy Staff They Comfort Me

True story…There lived a mother in a small South Carolina town who had a nine-month-old boy. She returned to work, entrusting him to the church daycare center several hours a day. She brought him home one afternoon during his first week at the center and found bruises on his buttocks and back when she changed his diaper. She immediately rushed the infant to the family physician, a general practitioner.

The doctor was in a quandary. The injuries were obvious, and the mother's story was credible. The law was clear. If he suspected abuse or negligent care, he was required to inform the South Carolina Child Protection Agency. An investigation was launched and a discovery was made that the daycare center believed that children had to have the devil beaten out of them!

Child Abuse Stats

According to the U.S. Department of Health and Human Services Children's Bureau, each day in the United States, more than three children die as a result of child abuse in the home. In 1998, an estimated 1,100 children died of abuse and neglect—an average of more than three children per day.

Most of the children who die are younger than five years old.

Of these fatalities, more than three-quarters were under the age of five; 38 % of the children were under the age of one.

More children (age four and younger) die from child abuse and neglect than any other single, leading cause of death for infants and young children. This includes falls, choking on food, suffocation, drowning, residential fires, and motor vehicle accidents.

In today's overprotective and abused society, the word *discipline* brings about different thoughts. To some, it brings up thoughts about abusive, mean, dictatorial parents or agencies with whips, switches, and closets. So in order to insure that no child is abused some go to the other extreme and *overprotect* and rush to outlaw anyone spanking any child for any reason. For some believe that adults have not the ability to administer corporal punishment with skill. Although I disagree with the assumption that there is never a need to spank, I understand the desire to protect children. In my family, we all grew up with one aunt whom we were all afraid of. Not the healthy fear and respect that children should possess of adults and other authorities in their lives, but a fear that made you pray that no one left you in the room with her alone. For when you were alone in the room with her, she would pinch you and ask us mean questions like "Why did you come over here?" and "When are you leaving?" Her son, my cousin whom I loved, and I were like David and Jonathan of the Old Testament, and the beatings he used to get under the name of discipline for simply doing boy things were cruel. To this day, he can be as cruel as he can be kind and I believe that his mother shaped much of that side of his character with her abusive discipline.

Another example of discipline gone badly is what happened at Oprah Winfrey's Leadership Academy for Girls in Johannesburg, South Africa. It was a school created to give young girls a safe place to live and go to school. A Johannesburg newspaper revealed that the matron grabbed a girl by the throat and threw her against a wall, all for the purpose of disciplining her for unacceptable behavior.

Discipline in its truest form, is a system of instruction used to teach and train another.

If this is what comes to mind as you read the word *discipline* in this chapter, rest assured that the above mentioned type of discipline is not what I am speaking of, nor do I support it. I am speaking of *discipline* in its truest form, a system of instruction used to teach and train another, a system for shaping behavior and character and teaching social skills.

A healthy system of instruction or discipline is well thought out and is based on best practices and is research based. A healthy system of discipline has a component of pleasure for reward; punishment for correction; protection for safety; and guidance for development.

However, in a good system of discipline, there is punishment. But each punishment benefits the end goal of the one being trained. Punishment in a good system of discipline is not the fruit of anger or revenge, but rather it is the fruit of love for someone you love. Let's begin at some foundational elements of a good discipline plan, and how when properly administered, it can provide our sons with a sense of safety, security, and hope. For without a true loving system of discipline, how can our sons ever find comfort in this world? For believe it or not, discipline is a source of comfort.

> Even though I walk through the valley of the shadow of death, I will fear no evil, for you are with me; your rod and your staff, they comfort me (Psalm 23:4).

Thy Rod and Thy Staff, They Comfort Me

In 2006 I served as the president of a local school board along with four other committed community workers.

Before our board was appointed, the previous board and its management company were having major problems with its school authorizer. The problems ranged from mismanagement to student behavior. Due to the controversy, the organization that authorized the charter for the school placed the school on a Plan of Correction (POC).

There were tasks in the POC such as: implementing a new accounting system, filing financial reports in a timely manner, administering prescribed professional development training to all teachers, and forming a new parent group.

The POC laid out systematically how we were to address the issues that were before us. More importantly, the POC addressed in detail, the punishments the authorizer would levy for not adhering to each step in the POC—punishments that ranged from fines to termination. One of our first important meetings as school board members was held for parents and staff to come ask questions and to hear our vision for the school. After we explained the task, structure, systems, and punishments of the POC, there was an overwhelming and collective sigh of relief and sense of comfort in the room. Not that anyone wanted to see anyone punished, but teachers, parents and students alike were comforted that systems for correction, accountability, and clear expectations were in place.

I would like to say that due to the maturity and intelligence of the members of the board, we needed no such motivation as a list of things that could happen if we did not follow the prescriptions in the POC, but that would not be true. The awareness of a real life rod or consequences was key in keeping everyone focused on the task at hand. As a matter of fact, without the rod of the authorizer, the parents of the school had no hope of us carrying out our promises.

Youth, especially boys are the same way; they need predictable, consistent structure. They need a systematic plan of instruction that details boundaries and the rod of correction when they cross them. Boys need to know four key answers for any good discipline plan to have lasting positive effects. Boys need to know answers to these questions:

1) What are the rules?
2) What are the consequences?
3) Who's going to administer the consequences?
4) Do you love me?

Rule #1—What Are The Rules?

Zig Ziglar, the famous motivational speaker, used to pick someone from the audience, show them a target, blindfold them, spin them around and say, "Now hit the target." After a few unsuccessful attempts, he would then say, "If you think that is hard, try hitting a target you don't have!" That's what it is like for a kid who has not been given the rules for living with you. Although you have the target, they have no target to shoot for. Occasionally, boys will hit the target, but most often they will miss it. How unfair is that for a kid when parents have unknown, non-verbalized expectations? How unfair is it to be punished for not hitting your parents' target when you never saw the target? Can you imagine standing at the throne of judgment and God saying, "My child, why did you continually commit the sin of eating chocolate cake?"

Secondly, how fair is it to be punished for not hitting a target that keeps moving? Today you can have chocolate cake but next year it is a sin. In counseling sessions with teens, I have found that one of the biggest seasons of struggles with their parents comes when parents go to church and get saved, and Christ becomes their Lord and Savior. Now this should begin a season of joy, but oftentimes it is not. For all of their young life they have seen Mom and Dad party, curse, and fight, but on Monday morning the rules drastically changed. However, no one calls a family meeting and informs the kids of this new way of life, the reason why, or what the new rules are.

Lastly, although we can't think of every situation that our sons will bring to us, there are some common and usual mistakes or choices that boys will make to get themselves in trouble. There are some basic areas of development that we should want our discipline plan to address. So for those areas, we can be proactive and lay down the rules.

A proactive plan of discipline should at least have rules and expectations for the following areas:

- Educational performance
- Spiritual growth
- Behavioral performance
- Family responsibility

The following are a couple of questions that you can ask yourself about the rules in your plan of discipline:

1. Does my son know what the rules are for education or are they vague such as "education is important"?
2. Does my son know what the rules are for his spiritual growth?
3. Does my son know what the rules are for his behavior?
4. Does my son know his responsibility to the family?

A plan of discipline or discipleship with rules that deal with these areas of development brings comfort.

Rule #2—What are the consequences?

An attorney friend of mine has a law library in his home and while visiting, I asked him why he had so many books. His reply was, "In these books are not only the laws that govern society but the punishments for each law that is broken." Now by no means am I suggesting that we parents have a list of punishments for every childish infraction. But what I am suggesting is that there be some consistent consequences that are well communicated, universal, humane, and age appropriate for breaking your rules.

> I am suggesting that there be some consistent consequences that are well communicated, universal, humane, and age appropriate for breaking your rules.

The two most important words of the previous statement are *consistent* and *consequences*. The execution of *consistent consequences* is very important to the validity and health of your plan of discipline. If there is no consistency, there will be no respect for your plan or any of the rules that you have put in place. Plain and simple! A healthy system of discipline will be consistent in rewarding and punishing a boy's behavior. The consistency not only validates, but reinforces the philosophies and practices that you want to convey to your son. The old saying that "repetition is the mother of learning" speaks to the heart of the why you must be consistent. If we want our sons to know to take off their shoes before they walk on the carpet, then we must be consistent in reminding them, praising them, and punishing them when applicable. How fast would we drive if the highway patrol were not consistent with at least the threat of consequences for speeding? How often would we pay the IRS if they were not consistent with consequences? I have been married for many moons now, and I can't count the number of times that I have told my wife "I love you," but for some reason she still wants me to be consistent or there will be consequences. Think of it this way: *consistent consequences help to create consistency!*

When *consequences* are consistent, communicated [verbally and written], universal (fair for all siblings), age appropriate, and humane, they help to keep us away from responding to our boys when we are angry. This type of proactive parenting limits the reports of child abuse that is so rampant today.

Rule #3—Who is going to administer the consequences?

One of the things that my parents' generation loves to romanticize is how "back in the day" if one of them got into trouble at school they would get punished by the principle, and then by parents when they got home. It did not stop there. A neighbor had the right to punish you if they caught you in the wrong and then you got it again when you got home. Obviously, in their day, every responsible adult had the right to administer consequences on the spot. They did not have to call to get parental permission and no one called the police. The philosophy was if an adult had to correct a child, the child had to have done something wrong. Period. This method of community and parental partnership for discipline was well understood by parents and youth alike. The partnership was responsible for keeping everybody safe and it communicated to all youth what the expectations were. Believe it or not, this informal community and parental partnership made life safe, predictable, and comfortable.

Today, that relationship has been blurred, bruised, broken, and some might say it has been buried since communities and parents don't work together anymore to raise the children. Because of this reality, we have communicated to our youth that the bulk of the responsibility to administer consequences falls on the parents and no one else. This reality is hardest on the single mother who has to do it all, all the time. However, the single mother must be ready and willing to also enforce her plan, for no plan can change or shape a son's behavior if it does not have someone to enforce its rules.

In our homes, we must be clear who has the authority and the duty to administer discipline. Is it the mother, father, or is it all of the above? This communication is critical so that everyone knows from which direction consequences can come. Also, it communicates order, premeditation, and self-control. This is especially important if you have remarried and two families are now blended.

The right and duty to administer consequences is also transferable to another responsible, well-controlled person such as a big brother, sister, babysitter, or family member who understands age appropriate consequences and the end goal that you have for your son. Someone who also knows that discipline is for training not just punishment. One of the mistakes that we men often make when we re-marry is thinking that we can administer punishment instantly before we have established a relationship or communicated with the children's parent about our philosophies or listened to theirs.

Rule #4—Do you love me?

One of the fruits of love is discipline, for true love corrects and those whom we love we discipline—we disciple, we train, and we teach. However, someone (probably a boy) once said, "I don't care how much you know, if I don't know how much you care!"

Our sons know intimately how cold and unloving the world is. They know the street and jungle code of "Only the strong survive," and in their journey to become a "man," they know all too well how callous life can be. However, our

> "I don't care how much you know, if I don't know how much you care!"

goal as loving parents is not to see how much pain they can endure; our plan of discipline in not a "boot-camp" so we can put our boots on their backsides when they error. Our discipline plan is for shaping the next generation of men. Our discipline plan must build men who know love and how to love. Men who will provide, protect, pray, and partner with their wives to multiply godly families in the earth. Therefore, we must let them know that we are doing what we do because we love them. We are doing to our sons what God does to all of us; for whom He loves, he disciplines (Proverbs 3:12).

Lastly, let me say that there is only one place in which the above rules, one through three, exist in a discipline plan and the fourth one does not. Prison! Thy rod and *thy staff* they *comfort me.* The staff of a good shepherd is a longer rod. It is used for stability and support when walking, especially up steep hills. This is where we get the word *staff* that is used to speak of those who assist us in the workplace. My staff at my office is a great example of what the shepherd in the field used his staff for—support! This is what we are to our boys. In a world where many things change constantly, we are to offer stable support. For example, in many schools I work in, one of the unfortunate occurrences in a child's life is the instability of the home. It sometimes appears that in one school year, many youth have moved at least four to five times. This is not stability and it does not bring comfort. It is very difficult for parents to be supportive to their children if things are always changing for them. For a child to be in comfort, his environment has to be supportive, stable, and predictable. He must have a sense of what is about to happen and who will be in his life when he arrives home.

This Is My Son In Whom
I am Well Pleased

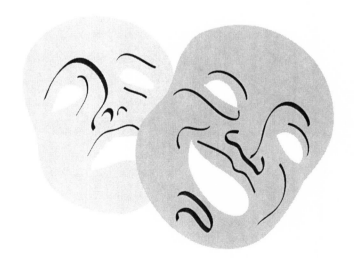

CHAPTER 14

The "Joy" of a Boy With Purpose

This Is My Beloved Son...

There is an old saying that love is blind. And 1 Peter 4:8 says, "...love covers over a multitude of sins." These two sayings are proven true in a good way and in a bad way when it comes to the power of parental love.

In a bad way, parents often are blind to the sins of their very own children because they love them so much. They love them so much that they literally blank out when correction comes in their children's directions.

In a bad way, again, parents use their love to cover or justify the sins that their child has committed and is still committing.

A parent whose love is blinding will watch the news and hear a report on youth behavior and agree with the report, criticizing "those" youth who act that way, and yet be blind to her own child's similar behavior. This blinding love will prevent a parent's ears and eyes from seeing the child in examples that the preacher is giving in his sermon about disobedient children—even when the sermon speaks to the exact behavior that a parent's child is exhibiting.

One of my duties as Board President on a local school board is to conduct disciplinary hearings for students who have been recommended for suspension from school. In all the time I have served in this capacity, I have only witnessed two parents who were not angry with the committee for carrying out their duty. All the other parents were angry with the board. These same angry parents would, however, be angry with the school if negative behavior from other children were allowed to exist in their children's learning environment. For many different reasons, parents are angry with educators, but often the love they have for their child will not let them see that their child causes problems as well.

Another example of a bad way that love covers sins is how the priest, Eli, covered the sins of his sons. In 1 Samuel, we are told that Eli's sons were corrupt and took meat that was supposed to be sacrificed to God. In addition, they slept with the women who served at the entrance to the Tabernacle of Meeting. Their conduct was so bad that it caused many to loose their faith in God; for what God would allow this? It was also recorded that Eli the priest knew of his son's deeds and did nothing! He covered their evil with his love.

More recently, we had the Columbine High School massacre that occurred on Tuesday, April 20, 1999. Two students, Eric Harris and Dylan Klebold, embarked on a shooting rampage killing twelve students and a teacher, as well as wounding twenty-three others before committing suicide. This tragedy remains the fourth-deadliest school killing in United States history, after the 1927 Bath School disaster, 2007 Virginia Tech massacre and the 1966 University of Texas massacre.

The massacre started debates regarding gun control laws, the availability of firearms in the United States, and gun violence involving youths. Much discussion also centered on the nature of high school cliques, subcultures, and bullying, as well as the role of violent movies and video games in American society. The shooting also resulted in an increased emphasis on school security, and a moral panic aimed at goth culture, social pariahs, the gun culture, the use of pharmaceutical anti-depressants by teenagers, violent films and music, teenage internet use, and violent video games.

However, all throughout the conversations and investigations, there were very few comments about parental correction from the parents of Eric Harris and Dylan Klebold. Their response was a cover of love for their sons who had taken their own lives in the massacre and anger at the outside forces that drove them to commit the act. Only the parents of the slain students displayed pain or offered suggestions of correction and prevention towards Eric and Dylan.

However, what a blessing it would have been for the rest of us parents if we could have heard a plea for parental wisdom and discipline from Eric and Dylans parents so we could prevent our sons from the state of mind that led to the killings. In the midst of their healing, how much more could they have helped us understand what we parents should pay attention to and prioritize with our sons?

In a good way, love is blind to undue criticism and negative reports that suggest that one child's potential is limited. Such as the mother of two sons who was told that her boys were learning disabled. This mother's love blinded her to the report and she would not believe that her sons could not learn. Her love challenged her sons to read and submit book reports to her each month even though she could not read herself. The reading led one of her sons to discover his gift and talent in the world of science, and as they say, the rest is history.

Her son went on to become a world-renowned pediatric neurosurgeon and a mentor to countless individuals of all ages. Her son, Benjamin S. Carson Sr., M.D., carries with him a message of hope for and faith in the human spirit and the remarkable ability of the human brain. To all who say that circumstances in their lives have made personal success impossible, Dr. Carson, director of pediatric neurosurgery at the Johns Hopkins Medical Institution, is living proof that perseverance, prayer, a mother's discipline, combined with blind love, can cover limitations and overcome most obstacles.

In Whom I am Well Pleased!

As parents, we all love our sons, even when they do wrong,

that's what Agape love is all about. It is unconditional, it is often unearned, and for the most part you can't lose it. That is the nature of a mother's love for her son. What good mother, if asked if she loved her son, would say, "No, I don't love him"? However, ask that same mother is she is *well pleased* with her son, and you might uncover a different story. You may have to take a seat and wait a while so that mother can exhale.

Understanding this distinction between loving a son and being *well pleased* with a son's behavior or attitude has allowed me to help many parents I counsel. Many parents are wrestling with why they have this battle between their hearts and minds regarding

> "Son, I love you, but there are many days that I don't like you!"

their sons. During counseling sessions with their sons, many parents have said, "Son, I love you, but there are many days that I don't like you!"

How is it that we parents can love a son that oftentimes we don't like?

The answer is, sometimes we have *a beloved son in whom we are not well pleased!* The million-dollar question becomes: how can we love our sons and, at the same time, be well pleased with them? I believe there are two ways.

One way not only pleases us as parents, it is the foundational key to all learning. The other is more personal unique to each child.

I am Well-Pleased When…

First, let us look at the foundational key to pleasing parents (drum roll please). And the answer is *obedience!* Yes, the dreaded word that twenty-first century adults and youth hate—*obedience.* However, *obedience* is the key that opens the door to eternal blessings. *Obedience* is the soil needed in order to plant the seeds of information. Without *obedience,* learning cannot take place. You see, parents have the responsibility of being a child's first teacher, but without a child first learning how to *obey,* how could a parent train a child to achieve even simple goals? Without first training our sons to obey us, how could we ever fulfill our Deuteronomy 6:6–7 responsibility?

These commandments that I give you today are to be upon your hearts. Impress them on your children. Talk about them when you sit at home and when you walk along the road, when you lie down and when you get up.

However, from the foundation of *obedience,* parents can begin to train on all levels. Trust me on this one; *obedience* is the foundational key to victory and peace in all of our households. If you disagree, just allow the opposite of obedience to rule and reign at your address.

What would have happened if:

- A certain son named Tiger would have disobeyed his parents and not picked up his golf clubs and practiced each and every day?

- Children of Asian heritage disobeyed their parents and did not study, could they be only 4% of the US population yet 25% of students on the campuses of our Ivy League schools?

- A certain son named Jesus was not obedient to his father to the point of death; would there have been salvation for mankind?

"Honour thy father and thy mother," is one of the commands spoken from Mount Sinai. It is the only one of the ten to which a promise is attached: "That thy days may be long upon the land which the Lord thy God giveth thee" (Exodus 20:12, KJV). Jesus is the Son of God; yet the Bible record tells us that he was obedient to his earthly parents, Joseph and Mary. In others words, He did as he was told, even when the task assigned him was not agreeable to his feelings.

Consider the nature and the necessity of obedience. Children are not always taught this important lesson and connection. They don't know why they should obey, and most of us can't tell them. We say, "Because I said so," and that settles it. Children must learn to submit to their parents; they must be trained and educated why they should. One reason is no one can be truly good for mankind who has not learned to yield his will, first to his parents. Obeying parental authority is the practice field for leadership. Those who learn to obey are the only ones who will be fit to command.

By learning the lesson of obedience, children are not only honoring their parents and lightening their burdens, but they are pleasing one higher in authority. "Honor thy father and thy mother" is a positive command. Children who treat their parents with disrespect, and disregard their wishes, not only dishonor them, but also break the law of God. The earlier the "will" is made to yield to the will of the parents, the less difficult it will be to yield to the requirements of God.

> The earlier the "will" is made to yield to the will of the parents, the less difficult it will be to yield to the requirements of God.

It amazes me how many of us parents miss this basic rule. Children must obey their parents, and they must learn to do so early in their development. Obedience does not start with big things at age fourteen; it starts with "No you can't sleep with Mom and Dad," "No you can't have that," and "Yes you will eat this." Then it progresses to "Pick up your clothes, brush your teeth, take the garbage out, eat your food and get dressed for church."

Our conversations and convictions should be saying that obedience is not up for debate; you will obey me for this is right and it is the first commandment with a promise! Also, we should not wait for some great organization to prove it's good for our sons to obey. We don't need a longitudinal study that proves what we already know. Children must obey their good and godly parents! It is non-negotiable. This principle is vitally important for single moms raising boys since when her sons get older, she must be ready for what I call the "Young Lion vs. Old Lion" confrontation.

If mom waits too late to establish her authority and the reason why obedience to authority is important to order and safety, her son will not be a son who is *well pleasing.* In addition, if a son does not learn obedience in his own home, the son won't be properly prepared to take on the task of independent flight and acceptance into society. Who wants students who won't obey the rules? Who wants employees who won't obey? What happens to adults who don't obey society's laws?

However, if a beloved son learns to obey righteous authority *promptly*, *properly*, and *pleasantly,* his parents will be well pleased indeed, and so will society! Sons like this could subdue the world, or at least bring joy to it.

I am Well-Pleased When...

The second way we parents can be *well pleased* with our sons is when we can see that their lives have direction and purpose. We are well pleased when we can see the potential that lies beneath coming to the surface and our sons show us signs that they finally get it—the light bulb is on!

Those of us who study or work with boys today are often puzzled by their choices and behaviors. We often wonder if they know that they are jeopardizing and sabotaging their future. Do they know that their current path leads to survival or death and not excellence? Do they know that their lives are gifts to mankind? Do they know that it was no mistake that they were born and that they have an assignment from God? Do they know that they are not just wandering generalities, but powerful meaningful specifics? Don't they know that they have purposes?

> When life has no purpose, then there is no purpose for life.

Why is having purpose in life so powerful for our sons? Because *when life has no purpose, then there is no purpose for life.*

When there is no purpose for life, self-destruction and depression is always at our son's doorstep. Let me prove how serious it is for a man to walk around on earth with power and potential, but no purpose.

The news reported that ex-heavyweight boxing champion Mike Tyson has been sentenced to twenty-four hours in jail and 360 hours of community service for drug possession and driving under the influence. The former champion who once was so out of control in the ring that he bit off the ear of his opponent Evander Holyfield, also received three years of probation after being caught driving with possession of cocaine. Tyson, now forty-one, was caught by police driving erratically leaving a nightclub. During a roadside search, they found three bags of cocaine and he later admitted to having used marijuana that day along with an anti-depressant.

In 1986, Tyson became the youngest heavyweight champion in history at twenty years of age. His potential was unknown and seemed unlimited. However, due to lack of a meaningful purpose to direct him, in 2003 he declared bankruptcy, having squandered an estimated fortune of 300 million! Myles Monroe brings it home when he says, "The greatest tragedy in life is not death, but life without a reason. It is dangerous to be alive and not know why you were given life." Although, over the years there have been many who have come to support and love Mike Tyson for the unforgettable moments and excitement that he brought back to boxing, it is very hard for any to say, "I am well pleased with the purpose and direction of his life."

But when our sons come to understand foundationally that all life has potential and purpose, we are all that much safer. And best of all, when our sons discover the purpose for their very own lives, the world itself will be blessed!

Is it possible to believe that, in today's society filled with wrong purpose and no purpose, our sons could grow up believing that their life is meant for a specific good? I say yes! However, it first takes parents who understand themselves, that their son is not a mistake nor is he a purposeless mass produced child. He was born with what I call a *universal and unique purpose* for his life.

Our sons' *universal purpose* as well as ours was stated in Mark 12:30:

" 'Love the Lord your God with all your heart, with all your soul and with all your mind and with all your strength.' And the second is this: 'Love your neighbor as yourself.' "

This says it all, and it has nothing to do with one's talents, gifts, wealth, height, weight, eye color, family tree, gender, or educational background. Everyone should have this as his or her purpose. That's why it's universal.

Finally, our boys need a *Unique Purpose*—one that is their guiding light for meaning and motivation on life's journey. A purpose that is bigger than the belief systems of superiority and racism, a purpose that does not contradict his *universal purpose*.

The book of Mark records Jesus as one knowing His purpose when He said, "Let us go into the next towns, that I may preach there also, *because for this purpose I have come forth.*" What if our sons matured to the point where they would say:

- ❑ *For this purpose* I have come to school
- ❑ *For this purpose* I play basketball
- ❑ *For this purpose* I obey my parents
- ❑ *For this purpose* I date

- ❏ *For this purpose* I don't do drugs
- ❏ *For this purpose* I don't have premarital sex
- ❏ *For this purpose* I am going to college
- ❏ *For this purpose* I love all my neighbors as myself
- ❏ *For this purpose* I don't waste my money
- ❏ *For this purpose* I won't be violent
- ❏ *For this purpose* I chose this type of friend

A son who understands that he has a *unique purpose* in not easily devalued in life, is not easily led astray by every new scheme and temptation. A son that knows his *unique purpose* is not driven by a pursuit of success so shallowly defined by monetary and material riches, but rather by the pursuit of what I call *personal success*—the maximizing of one's own potential. This is the type of son whom a parent loves, is *well pleased* with and is a joy to be around!

CHAPTER 15

The Conclusion of the Matter

In Ecclesiastes 12:13–14 Solomon ends his findings by writing this:

> Now all has been heard; here is the conclusion of the matter: Fear God and keep his commandments, for this is the whole *duty* of man. For God will bring every deed into judgment, including every hidden thing, whether it is good or evil.

These words are so powerful that every book ever written or to be written could end this way. For at the end of the day, if *The Pains & Joys of Raising Boys* assisted in any small way to leading our sons to fear God and keep his commandments, then we all have succeeded. I have succeeded by writing and you for reading. The challenge now is that you won't be like most twenty-first century learners and be note rich and application poor. Therefore, I encourage you to do with this book what my parents told me while at the dinner table: take what you need, but eat what you take.

My prayer for us all is for us to commit, count the costs, and then go out and conquer. I pray that we will first *commit* to family, for God is a family God, which is why the good Father sent His Son to save His brothers and sisters, and why we can cry out "Abba, Father."

I pray that we would stop and *count the costs* of the millions of abandoned, hurting, feminized, fatherless, uneducated, incarcerated, and drug addicted sons. Then ask ourselves if we should continue to apply these worldly solutions when a heavenly one is needed, ready—and waiting.

Lastly, I pray that we would someday, sometime soon lift our heads up, leave the safety of our homes and churches, and go out into the world; conquer and have dominion as we were commanded to do. I pray that we would go and make disciples of all our sons. Baptize them in the name of the Father, and of the Son, and of the Holy Spirit, and teach our sons to obey everything God has commanded them.

For surely I am with you always, to the very end of the age (Matthew 28:30).

—Jesus

CHAPTER 16

A Personal Letter to All Fathers

In the last entry of the adventures of our favorite Kryptonian, Superman comes back to earth. The movie's plot is: Superman returns to earth after leaving us for five years. He left us unprotected to go on a personal journey. He left us unprotected from those who would take advantage of us. He left us unprotected without even saying goodbye.

However, when Superman returned home to Metropolis, fear left. When Superman returned home, doubt left. When Superman returned home, the citizens' protection from evil returned home. When Superman returned home, so did hope! Can you see where I am going with this? For now, the only real life Superman in my son's world is me, for now. I am faster than a speeding bullet that may hurt or harm him. For now, I am the one able to leap tall buildings or problems that he may face. For right now, I am his provider and protector.

After leaving the movie with my son, I asked myself two questions:

1) What would happen if I left the home of my son for five years for any reason?

2) What would happen if the real Super-Men returned home to their children?

The answer to question number one is, my wife, mother in-law, mother, and son would be devastated. Regardless of what I said, how often I picked him up on the weekend, or how much money they took from my check, my son would not be the same. He could not call out to me in the night, or run to me in the next room with his concerns. He could not be the same as if I were at the same address raising him. If he would be the same, that means my being at the same address means nothing.

Now to question number two: What if the real Super-Men returned home to their children?

1. Mothers would stop crying.
2. Babies would stop crying.
3. Mothers would not have to work so hard, and so often.
4. Mothers would not have to have so many different men in their lives.
5. Our sons would grow up seeing the correct model for family.
6. Grandmothers would not have to be mothers again.

7. Grandparents would not have to be broke in their golden years.

8. Young men would not feel the powerful need for gangs.

9. Our daughters would know what a real man does for his family.

10. Ours boys would surely be joys and not pains.

Will the real Super-Men please come home!

Bibliography

Chess, Stella and Alexander Thomas. *Know Your Child: an authoritative guide for today's parents*. New York: Basic Books, 1987.

Clark, Chap. *Hurt: inside the world of today's teenagers*. Grand Rapids: Baker Academic: 2004.

Cosby, Bill. *Fatherhood*. Boston: Hall, 1987.

Davis, Sampson, Rameck Hunt and George Jenkins. *The Pact*. New York: The Berkley Publishing Group, Penguin Group, 2002.

Dobson, James C. *The New Dare To Discipline*. Wheaton, Ill: Tyndale House Publishers, 1992.

Donne, John. *Meditation XVII*. 19 August 2004. November 2007, http://isu.indstate.edu/ilnprof/ENG451/ISLAND/

Farrar, Steve. *King Me*. Chicago: Moody Publishers, 2005.

Farrar, Steve with Dave Branon. *Point Man: taking new ground*. Sisters, OR: Multnomah Books, 1996.

Grossman, Dave and Gloria DeGaetano. *Stop Teaching Our Kids to Kill.* New York: Crown Publishers, 1999.

Gurian, Michael. *The Wonder of Boys.* New York: Putnam, 1996.

Hyles, Jack. 2 December 1973. January 2008, http://www.jesus-is-savior.com/

James, Sr., Rev. Clarence Lumumba. *Lost Generation? Or Left Generation!* Youth Leadership Development Programs, 2004.

Jones, Adam. *Case Study: The Armeian Genocide, 1915–1917.* Gendercide.org. Gendercide Watch, 1999–2002. January 2008, http://www.gendercide.org/case_armenia.html

King, Dr. Martin Luther. *The Measure of a Man.* Philadelphia: Fortress Press, 1988.

Lewis, G. Craig. *The Truth About Hip-hop.* (Video series)

McCall, Nathan. *Makes Me Wanna Holler: A Young Black Man in America.* New York: Random House, 1994.

McDowell, Josh. *Beyond Belief to Convictions.*
Wheaton, Illinois: Tyndale House Publishers, 2002. *p 5.*

O'Reilly, Bill. *Talking Points: Birth Control Pills for 11-Year-Old Girls... 19 October 2007. November 2007,* http://www.foxnews.com/story/0,2933,303521,00.html

Parenting Issues. Homosexual Parenting: Is It Time for a Change? American College of Pediatricians, 2004. http://www.acpeds.org/American College of Pediatricians: 2004.

Powell, Alfred (Coach). *Hip Hop Hypocrisy.* iUniverse, Inc., 2006.

Roundy, B. *STD rates on the rise.* New York Blade News. p 1. 15 December 2000. 14 January 2008 <http://acpeds.org/

Steinem, Gloria. Interview by Colleen Casto and Mary Dickenson of *No Safe Place: Violence Against Women.* 14 January 2008, http://www.pbs.org/kued/nosafeplace/interv/steinem.html

Steyer, James P. *The Other Parent: the inside story of the media's effect on our children.* New York: Atria Books, 2002.

Stykes, Charles. *Dumbing Down Our Kids.* New York: St. Martin's Griffin, 1996.

Triplett, William. *Congress holds hearing on hip-hop.* Variety. 4 September 2007. 14 January 2008, http://www.variety.com/article/VR1117971328. html?categoryid=16&cs=1

Trostli, Roberto. *Rhythms of Learning: What Waldorf Education Offers Children, Parents & Teachers.* Hudson, NY: Anthroposophic Press, 1998.

Woods, Earl. *Playing Through.* New York: Harper Collins Publishers, 1998.

Endnotes

[1] Steinem, Gloria. Interview by Colleen Casto and Mary Dickenson of *No Safe Place: Violence Against Women*. 14 Januarty 2008, www.pbs.org/kued/nosafeplace/interview/steinem.html

[2] Hyles, Jack. 2 December 1973. January 2008, http://www.jesus-is-savior.com/Books,%20Tracts%20&%20Preaching/Printed%20Books/Dr%20Jack%20Hyles/unisex.htm

[3] *Parenting Issues. Homosexual Parenting: Is It Time for a Change?* American College of Pediatricians, 2004, http://www.acpeds.org/?CONTEXT=art&cat=22&art=50, American College of Pediatricians: 2004.

[4] Roundy, B. *STD rates on the rise.* New York Blade News. p 1. 15 December 2000. 14 January 2008, http://acpeds.org/?CONTEXT=art&cat=22&art=50

[5] Grossman, Dave and Gloria DeGaetano. *Stop Teaching Our Kids to Kill.* New York: Crown Publishers, 1999.

[6] Steyer, James P. *The Other Parent: the inside story of the media's effect on our children.* New York: Atria Books, 2002.

[7] Steyer, James P. *The Other Parent: the inside story of the media's effect on our children.* New York: Atria Books, 2002.

[8] Clark, Chap. *Hurt: inside the world of today's teenagers.* Grand Rapids: Baker Academic: 2004.

[9] Donne, John. *Meditation XVII.* 19 August 2004. November 2007, http://isu.indstate.edu/ilnprof/ENG451/ISLAND/

[10] O'Reilly, Bill. *Talking Points: Birth Control Pills for 11-Year-Old Girls...* 19 October 2007. November 2007, http://www.foxnews.com/story/0,2933,303521,00.html

[11] This "wise man" refers to my father.

[12] Farrar, Steve with Dave Branon. *Point Man: taking new ground.* Sisters, OR: Multnomah Books, 1996.

About The Author

CARLOS JOHNSON is founder of Back-2-The Family Ministries, and the co-creator of the personal development philosophy and program entitled *The I.M.A.G.E. Personal Success Failure Prevention System.*

In 1990 when he began talking about creating a philosophy and developing a system that teaches youth how to discover, plan, and train for the achievement of personal success, few people believed he would do it.

Now in the new millennium, *The I.M.A.G.E. Personal Success Failure Prevention System* is a reality, and I.M.A.G.E. of Success, Inc. has become a credible, proven organization in youth and family development.

Johnson's company utilizes his I.M.A.G.E. philosophy of personal success to help youth succeed by conducting seminars and workshops which cover areas such as: personal talent discovery, career planning, life management, and classroom management.

Today, the *I.M.A.G.E. Personal Success Philosophy and Failure Prevention System* is taught in school systems, juvenile detention facilities, religious institutions, and community organizations.

In an effort to prepare young adults for leadership and employment, Johnson opened the I.M.A.G.E. Personal Success Training Institute in Southfield, Michigan.

Johnson also conducts workshops for parents entitled **Power Paren-T-een Tips— "Strategies for Taking Back the Power."** *These* workshops help parents understand today's teens while helping teens understand today's parents.

Carlos Johnson's *Power Paren-T-een* experiences can be read weekly in local Michigan newspapers and daily in the *Prescriptions for the Parental Headaches.* Or you can listen to his newly released CD, *Power Paren-T-een.*

His personal battle cry is:

"Success is personal; therefore, everyone can achieve personal success!"

Carlos Johnson may be contacted for information or speaking engagements at **www.back2thefamily.org**

To order additional copies of *The Pains & Joys of Raising Boys*, or to find out about other books by Carlos Johnson please visit our website:

www.back2thefamily.org

A bulk discount is available when 12 or more books are purchased at one time.

For Speaking or Preaching Contact:

I.M.A.G.E. OF SUCCESS, INC.
at (888) 462-4324
or www.imageofsuccess.com

LaVergne, TN USA
12 March 2010
175765LV00002B/1/P